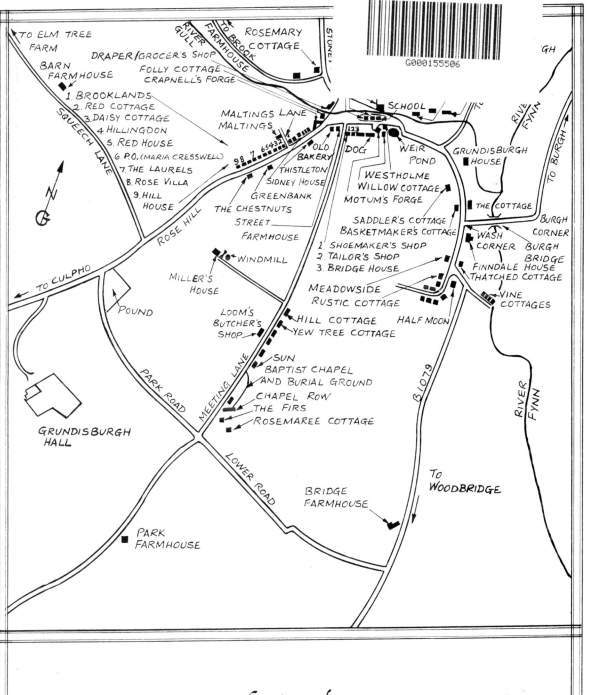

Centre of
Grundisburgh
about 1850

Grundisburgh

Grundisburgh's first car: Charles Cotton in his 1902 Benz.

Grundisburgh

THE HISTORY
OF A SUFFOLK VILLAGE

PETER BISHOP

SILENT BOOKS

For Helen

First published in Great Britain 1992
by Silent Books, Swavesey, Cambridge CB4 5RA

© text copyright Peter Bishop 1992

Each plate is reproduced with the permission of the present
owners

ISBN 1 85183 044 8

Typeset by Goodfellow & Egan, Cambridge
Printed in Great Britain by
Redwood Press Ltd, Melksham, Wiltshire

Jacket
Grundisburgh church and green, about 1900

Jacket flap
Grundisburgh's crocodile. (From the 1589 Manorial Survey)

Contents

Acknowledgements

(Numbers refer to illustrations)

Mr. Rodney Blois: 5, 10.

Lord Cranworth: 2, 6, 11, 13, 15, 30, 31, 32.

Rev. Norman Davis: 4, 7, 14, 16, 17.

Mr. John Dunnett: 19, 35, 39.

Mrs Hilda Finch: 33, 40.

Museum of East Anglian Life: 44, 45.

Mr. Claude Nunn: 28, 34.

Mr. George Pipe: 18, 22, 27, 37.

Mrs. Sylvia Pipe: 36, 41.

Mr. Douglas Shotton: 25, 26.

Wing Cmdr. and Mrs. Sowden: 46.

Suffolk Photographic Survey (Suffolk Record Office): 1, 3, 9, 20, 24, 29, 38, 42, 43.

Mr. R.C. Wilding: 21, 23.

Mr. Humphrey Lyttelton: copyright of extracts from George Lyttelton's letters.

Top Floor Studio, Woodbridge, has carried out much of the photographic work.

Illustrations

Foreword

THIS is a slim volume, one to be read on a wet afternoon or a
winter's evening, because Grundisburgh is a small place. Until
the 1970s, its population was barely double what it is thought to have
been before the Black Death. And its historical debris is correspond-
ingly sparse.

Even if there were more of it, how much would be worth relating?
When we meet our predecessors on the real Doomsday, how much
will we have in common except the mud and dust of Grundisburgh
with which they struggled daily to keep starvation at bay? Poverty,
like pain, is a boring business, repeatedly dragging back attention
from more interesting matters, and for the thirty-odd generations in
this history, it was the lot of almost everybody. Disease, too, was
ever in the background; and it is striking how many people, like
today, had several spouses, but following death rather than divorce.

We know that for centuries they were obsessed with witchcraft,
that many great events, wars for example, must have touched them
closely, and that once in nine hundred years something of real
significance must surely have happened in the village, but the records
are silent. What information we have is usually indistinct and always
haphazard, an amateur watercolour of a sea-mist, best taken in with a
quick blink. That is why I suspect this book, if it is worth reading at
all, may make more sense at a single sitting.

For me, random impressions stick in the mind. One, that of
Hervey de Bourges riding into the village after the Battle of
Hastings, lacks the clear evidence that he ever came to Grundisburgh
at all. Some are more reliable, like dear, snobbish William Blois
returning to Grundisburgh Hall after his honeymoon, or Alice
Driver prodded with a pitchfork, or Mr. Webster in his pulpit, or the
cartload of paupers being 'delivered' at the new workhouse. Others
relate to the actual documents more than to the events behind them,
such as James Upson's suicide note, or the piece of paper for which
William Worledge changed his last half-crown. Others, again,
acquire an extra dimension from photographs, the unexpectedly
mild face, for instance, of Mrs. Hardy.

This book will more than have fulfilled its purpose if it provides
the reader with a few similar impressions, disconnected fragments,
but better, I hope, than the weary gazetteers and genealogies which
so often pass for local history. Better the blurred voice of Tennyson
on the phonograph than to have no idea of it. Modern pressures have
all but destroyed the idea, the entity, of Grundisburgh. Hopefully it
is not too late to revive it.

It may be thought I have put too much emphasis on money, once
called man's greatest invention. I have always been interested in the
private details of other people's finance, and in the polite intercourse
of real life one gets little opportunity to find out. It provides such
precise evidence with which there can be no argument, a sixth sense,
as someone wrote, whose absence renders the other five unreliable.
For the historian it is an invaluable tool, but obviously one can
overdo it, and if I have, I apologise. Younger readers, to whom
pre-decimalised pence and shillings will be as alien as annas and
rupees, should refer to the final section of Chapter One. Throughout
the book 'pence' refers to the old currency.

I am aware of the quagmire to which adverbs can reduce any
narrative, but the three P's – perhaps, possibly and probably – are
difficult to avoid in a history like this without omitting a great deal
or being dishonest. They are the most intrusive when introducing
passages of whimsical speculation, of which I hope I am not too
guilty.

Future historians of the village may decide I should have left some
out, either because they were unnecessary or because what they
qualified was incorrect anyway. But at least my mistakes are no fault
of those on whom I have relied so much: Douglas Shotton, whose
scholarly work on the Victorian censuses and related matters has
saved me weeks, if not months, of labour; Lynda Bridges, Alison
Dillon, Robert and Nilda Lambert, Hilda Tuck and the many
contributors to the Grundisburgh Local History Magazines 1984–90;
and all the people who have most kindly helped and entertained me,
a newcomer, with their memories of the village, especially Mr. R.
Barclay, Mr. and Mrs J. Batchelor, Mr. K. Burch, Mr. J. Clarke,
Mrs. M. Derbyshire, the Rev. and Mrs. A.D. Drake-Brockman,
Mr. J. Dunnett, Mrs. H. Finch, Miss K. Gates, Mrs. M. Gentry,
Mrs. E. Harris, Mr. and Mrs. W. Lankester, Mrs. R. Leach, Mrs.
M. Lovett, Mr. C. Nunn, Mr. G. Pipe, Mrs. S. Pipe, Mrs. N. Scott,
Mr. and Mrs. R. Smith and Wing Cmdr. and Mrs. E. Sowden. In
addition I would like to thank the Rector, Norman Davis and Mr.
R.C. Wilding of the Baptist Chapel for their aid and encouragement.

I must also mention my gratitude to the staff of the Ipswich
Record Office for their unfailing assistance, and to Helen, my wife,
but for whose support and patience this book would never have been
completed.

Finndale House   *17 June 1992*

CHAPTER ONE

The Domesday Manors

GRUNDISBURGH: there are two theories about the origin of this curiously memorable name. Is it from the old Norse, Grundi, a ninth-century Viking who perhaps sailed up the then tidal river from Martlesham Creek and built his fort or burgh near the confluence of what the map now calls the Lark and the Gull? Or is it simply the ground (grund) below Burgh, the old Roman settlement to the north-east close to the main road, shorter and straighter than the A12, which linked Colchester and Dunwich? Coincidentally these alternatives are echoed in current pronunciation in the village, some people sounding the 'i' of Grundisburgh, and some not. (The '-burgh' rhymes with Peterborough or St. Petersburg according to taste.)

By the time of the Domesday Survey in 1086 the settlement, hardly yet a village, covered 640 acres, one-third the size of the present parish and almost certainly within its bounds. It was about 95 per cent arable, a clearing in the surrounding scrubland. Around and among the nucleus of its four manors, in large and probably hedgeless fields, were the villagers' holdings and the fifty or so huts where they lived; in general appearance not unlike a vast modern allotment area, dotted around with thatched toolsheds. Inheritance and a vague desire to ensure a fair distribution of good land and poor were gradually splitting up earlier blocks into scattered, less efficient strips on the open field plan which had long existed in the Midlands. It was one of those things which seemed a good idea at the time, but it was slowly ruining the peasants, a process hastened by the Aryan thoroughness of their new masters.

Around the settlement, on the poor ground on the edge of the woodland, grazed the plough oxen. There were 72 at the time of Domesday, 9 ploughteams, slightly fewer than twenty years before, together with a number of sheep, pigs and horses; surely hens as well, the peasants' universal friend, which are seldom mentioned in the Survey. The Domesday commissioners who calculated the village's acreage reckoned this grazing land was worthless and excluded it from their sums. All the animals of course were small by the standards of their twentieth-century descendants, as were their masters: the King himself, who was considered a tall man, was five foot ten.

The commissioners were unfamiliar with the social complexities of life in an English village and since they were not compiling a census, evidently didn't care. Bordars, villeins and freemen, the three classes mentioned in the Grundisburgh entries, were all the same to them, and 'villein' is used throughout the Survey as a generic term for villager. Indeed, it is probable the differences were not that great: everyone was free but some were more free than others. There were no longer slaves in the village, although they were still around elsewhere, one slave being worth two horses. The Normans were busy converting them into bordars, whose young and old would be less of a liability. Domesday lists 52 men in Grundisburgh, of whom 21 were bordars, 4 were villeins and 27 freemen. Including their families this indicates a population of 250.

Bordar (the lowest form of feudal life) and villein both owed their lord several days' labour a week, while the freeman, though owing no labour, had to purchase protection with hard cash, putting himself 'under commendation' (patronage) to any lord he hoped suitable. Before the Normans came, several men in Grundisburgh had had King Harold himself as patron, Harold as the commissioners curtly called him. A holding of 5 acres was regarded as subsistence level, and there was many a freeman whose holding was much less. He might try to hire out his labour to make ends meet, but work would have been hard to find with bordars and villeins doing it for nothing. The alternative, often taken, was to surrender his 'free' status and join them.

The high proportion of freemen was not exceptional for Suffolk (after Middlesex the most populous county) where manorial holdings were unusually small and there were more freemen than in the rest of England put together. War – the Viking raids over the two previous centuries – is a great leveller, as we have seen in our own times.

The policy of William the Conqueror was to change as little as possible, merely to drag the sleepy feudal system of the English into the eleventh century. Even so, he effected a revolution. The Normans were efficient and on the make. They despised the English and got every penny and every minute out of them that was their due. Where would it all end? Everywhere there was pressure, but the results came through: after twenty years of Norman rule, many people had become richer, but as always, the rich became richer faster. Revolutions are easier to bear in such times, but even in

Grundisburgh, far from the world's events, there must have been villagers who asked themselves if the quality of freedom, the quality of life, was what it had been in their fathers' day. The fact that the invasion had been blessed by the Pope must have been particularly galling to the more pious among them. Ipswich had a bad time after the Conquest: was Grundisburgh unaffected?

The Domesday Book, so called because its conclusions permitted no appeal, was compiled to find out what the country was worth on the basis of annual rental values (the answer, meaningless now, was over £73,000) and whether enough geld, or tax, was being paid. In the case of Grundisburgh, the commissioners reckoned that the pre-Conquest valuation was 112 shillings and 'now' 127 shillings, so the original geld of 15 pence looked a bit low. The domains of the four manors comprised 60 per cent of the Domesday acreage. The lord of the largest was evidently responsible for raising the tax and paying it to the collection point of the Carlford Hundred (the intermediary between manor and county) supposedly near the old Post Office, Hasketon. Grundisburgh's heavy clay soil, like rubber to plough, was thus valued at 2½ pence per acre, in the Grade II class.

The commissioners took evidence under oath not only from the lords of the manors or their agents, and from the French and English officials of the Hundred, but also from six men in each village. As it happens the Survey gives the names of precisely six Grundisburgh freemen: Burric, Ailric, Brown, Aluric, Brightman and Siric.

Burric and Ailric held just 5 acres between them, valued at 10 pence a year. They used to own 4 oxen, half a ploughteam, but latterly had lost them. Brown's valuation was reduced in the Survey from 5 shillings to 4. Even so, he seems to have remained one of the most prosperous men in the village with 20 acres of arable and 2½ acres of meadow. His meadow alone should have been worth around 4 shillings, so it looks as if he didn't sweat too much over the arable, having lost half his original team of 8 oxen. Aluric and Brightman shared 14 acres and had recently lost part-ownership of a plough-team. Their land was rated highly at 10 shillings, over 8 pence an acre. Siric had one acre.

The only other villagers named were Goodwin, Ulwin and Leuric, who were half-freemen, indicating they had divided loyalties and other duties elsewhere. They had recently lost all 4 of the oxen with which they had tilled their joint 7 acres, and their valuation had been slashed by half to 1 shilling. Perhaps their misfortunes or follies were being talked about at the time so that their names slipped by chance into the great Survey. Perhaps they were just a popular trio, a Saxon Marx Brothers.

The most important men to the people of Grundisburgh were obviously the lords of the four manors, two of whom were exceedingly grand and probably never came near the place: Earl Hugh of Chester and Roger de Poictu, the younger son of his neighbour on the Welsh border, the Earl of Shrewsbury. The other two manors were held by the man who really counted locally, Hervey de Bourges. He came from central France, one of the young landless knights (knight indicating nothing more than the ability to ride a horse) recruited by William to supplement the inadequate resources of Normandy. His reward was about twenty manors in Suffolk plus other bits and pieces. The two Grundisburgh manors seem to have comprised his largest unit, so it is possible he actually lived in the village, which would help explain why his larger manor (Bast's?) on whose land possibly the church was built, was the only one of the four to have increased in value.

The feudal theory was that all land belonged to the King, who granted it in exchange for an undertaking to provide so much military service when required. Hervey held his smaller manor as tenant-in-chief of the King and the larger as under-tenant of the Abbot of Ely. The latter was 150 arable acres worked by 2 villeins and 5 bordars with 2 ploughteams. A ploughteam was reckoned to cover an acre a day, so this amount of land represented up to three months' continuous work. In a hard winter they would have been pushed to complete it. The men also cultivated 4 acres for themselves with one ploughteam. There were 3 rouncies on the manor together with 6 cows, 16 pigs and 70 sheep. A rouncey is a farm-horse, distant ancestor of the Suffolk Punch. Hay was provided for this lot in winter from a 4-acre meadow, supplemented by the produce of a couple more on Hervey's other manor, which had no livestock apart from oxen. All the meadows were no doubt along the flood-plains of the two rivers. There were also 3 valuable hives of bees. The commissioners doubled the taxable value of this manor to £2 a year. Hervey's other manor (Grundisburgh Hall?) was of 120 acres and valued at 16 shillings. It was worked by 1 villein and 4 bordars with 1 ploughteam. The men had no land of their own but kept a ploughteam, presumably to hire out to the manor, which clearly needed another. Burric, Ailric and Brown came under this manor along with the three half-freemen.

The third manor, Earl Hugh's, was of 60 acres and assessed at 10 shillings. It was let to 4 freemen who had a villein and 2 bordars working under them. The domain, which looks overstaffed, also had a ploughteam and 2 acres of meadow.

The fourth manor, held by Roger de Poictu, was also of 60 acres with 3 bordars who for some years had worked it without the manor's own oxen. It was assessed highly at 15 shillings. The men had no land but 4 oxen of their own. De Poictu also held another 140 acres in separate parcels in the village which were let to an assortment of freemen including Aluric, Brightman and Siric.

No narrative of eleventh-century Grundisburgh would be complete without mention of the lords of the four manors who had dominated the village before the Conquest. The commissioners of Domesday methodically record the names of three of them, but their fate is unknown. If they were village people, rather than absentee landlords, it is possible they stayed on among the anonymous freemen or even villeins, ploughing for a Norman lord the fields on whose produce they themselves had once lived in some style. Of Hervey's two manors, the largest had been held from the Abbot of Ely by Algar, who, evidently to no avail, had also put himself under the Abbot's personal patronage. The second had been held by Goodrich under King Harold's patronage, as were the predecessors of Earl Hugh, an unnamed freeman and his wife. The holder of the fourth manor had been Brictnoth, also under the ineffectual patronage of the Abbot.

The English currency which had been in use for three centuries before the Battle of Hastings was based on the silver penny and the pound sterling: 12 pence to the shilling and 20 shillings to the pound, a system the Normans and their successors left totally unchanged until 1971. During those years inflation has made a nonsense of historical values. Only the crudest adjustments can provide some idea of real worth. For example, about the time of Domesday the basic agricultural wage was 1 penny a day in the old currency; a pound of butter cost ½ a penny and a dozen eggs a ¼ penny; while a hen, presumably a laying bird, cost 1 penny, which seems relatively dear. Wheat prices fluctuated greatly and only after a good harvest could the eleventh-century housewife have produced a 2 lb loaf for a ¼ penny. Keeping the sums very simple, it is possible to say food prices have risen by up to one thousand times between then and now, and labour by five thousand. One can either multiply eleventh-century prices by one thousand to obtain actual modern approximations or by five thousand to discover the comparable cost to a farm worker today, the factor of five between the multipliers representing in rough terms one aspect of his improved standard of living over 900 years.

The multiplier of five thousand seems appropriate also for land values: taking all Domesday Grundisburgh as a single farm of 600 acres, an assessment of about £6 then indicates a profitability of £30,000 a year now, a good but not impossible return. Against the vaiue of what he produces, the farmer, like the labourer, has improved his position. A higher crop yield is no doubt the chief explanation, the chemist rather than the social reformer. It is worth repeating that these figures are guides only; and a slight wobble or distortion in the early amounts can make a big difference to the multipliers.

Silver, on which the whole structure was founded – the pound being originally a pound's weight of the metal – has risen over thirty-fold in price, much of that in the twentieth century.

CHAPTER TWO

※

Wergen Hall

Hᴇʀᴠᴇʏ de Bourges seems to have had one surviving child, his heiress, Isilia, who around the turn of the century married a widower called William Peche. A knight like Hervey, he had not done so well out of the Conquest, perhaps because he was too young to have fought at Hastings. He was a retainer of the lord of Clare, Richard FitzGilbert, and held under him a couple of small properties at Dalham and Clopton near Clare as well as three other pieces of land elsewhere.

The Domesday commissioners, recalling the unfortunate derivation of his name, refer to him uncompromisingly as 'William the Sinner'. Is it too fanciful to ignore the erratic spelling of the period and trace a deliberate attempt on William's part to distance himself from what was at best a tedious joke, at worst an awkward reminder of some skeleton in the family cupboard? In any case Peche alters over the years to de Peche, Pecche, and (most ingeniously, indicating two syllables) Pecchie. One of his descendants who inherited Clopton cut the Gordian knot and changed his name to Clopton.

William's first wife had been a Saxon girl, Alfwen. She produced two boys, Simon and Ralph, about whom little is known except that they died childless. The succession of Isilia's children, Hamon and Basilia, was thus uncomplicated and Hamon inherited virtually everything including the land at Grundisburgh.

Hamon spent much time at Court, reportedly becoming a young favourite of the King, Henry I, who for the year 1130 remitted the geld on all the de Bourges property, whether for services rendered or as a result of whingeing, we don't know. Certainly at 28 shillings it looks onerous pro rata compared to the admittedly low charge of 15 pence on Grundisburgh. History doesn't relate whether Hamon, having been excused payment of the tax himself, went so far as to excuse the villagers under his control from paying him.

Like his father, he married an heiress who brought him a substantial property in Cambridgeshire valued at seven knights' fees; that is, she or her husband held the land subject to a promise to provide the King with the military service of seven knights if required. There was no tariff in such matters but a ratio between £5 and £10 worth of land a year per knight was common. As the de Bourges lands in Suffolk with their income of barely £40 owed the service of twelve knights, of whom Grundisburgh and Great Bealings owed one, the Conqueror appears to have struck a hard bargain with Hamon's grandfather.

It was a bargain that in the next generation his younger son, Gilbert (tactfully named after the family's patron) was to find a problem when he had to pay King John the hefty sums of £27 and £54 to avoid providing the requisite assistance.

Gilbert's son, young Hamon, who came as a teenager into his inheritance, not surprisingly supported the barons against the King over Magna Carta. Thereafter he married a foreign girl, Eve (i.e. not English or French) by whom he had six sons, evidently a formidable gang, 'powerful, prudent and strong', according to a contemporary account. Although Gilbert, the eldest, inherited the lion's share, Hugh, the third brother, didn't do too badly, receiving lands near Clare, Martley Hall at Easton plus the manors of Great Bealings and Grundisburgh. That was in 1241, when he was still a very young man.

Hugh and his wife Ide lived to begin with at Martley Hall until the marriage of their daughter Margery, who got that manor as her dowry. After that they may have settled in Grundisburgh; certainly in 1302 their son and heir, another Hugh, was living in the village. They began to rebuild the family church and in 1285 established a Tuesday market and a fair in Whitsun week, both nice little money spinners. Village greens are rare in this part of Suffolk, and this commercial venture may have been the origin of Grundisburgh's and the reason for its survival. If Hervey de Bourges had occupied the house of the larger manor (now Bast's?) at some stage the family had moved up the hill to the land held directly from the King. The latter was known by this time as Wergen Hall, the house by the willows, near or under the present site of Grundisburgh Hall.

The precise extent of Hugh's property and the village as a whole remains uncertain. Domesday gives the dimensions of the village as 1¼ miles by ¾, and one might guess it stretched from roughly the present domain of Grundisburgh Hall as its western limit to the river Lark as its eastern. Lower Road would have skirted its southern edge. As one might expect, the church would be approximately in the middle of the parish. Great Common Field was to the east of Meeting Lane and fields either side of Stoney Road show signs of the old strip cultivation.

Hugh's land might have been more extensive than Hervey's. The

Wergen Hall? Note the kennel. (From the St. Christopher mural.)

population of the village had probably doubled since the Conquest, and with more mouths to feed, the surrounding scrub and woodland would have been cleared for arable or sheep-pasture especially to the north, up to the parish boundaries as we know them today.

By this time the two small Domesday manors, those of Earl Hugh and Roger de Poictu, had apparently disappeared, either split up or absorbed by the two now-combined manors of the Peches'. Four manors and four manorial courts in one village would have been administratively untidy and doubtless irritating to the lord of the largest of them. The manorial court which sat once every three weeks existed chiefly to enforce the lord's rights, not only in rent and labour due but also in a whole battery of feudal rackets – merchate, heriot, chevage and so on – which forbade any villager from dying, inheriting, moving, marrying off a daughter, even living outside the village, without asking permission and paying for it. The court also settled boundary disputes and punished brawling and similar offences, keeping the fines.

Young Hugh succeeded his father in 1292, and dying childless was himself followed briefly in 1310 by Eva, his twice-widowed elder sister. From her first husband she had received a bleak little property at Eriswell near Mildenhall, and there she remained during her second marriage to a neighbour of her parents, Robert de Tuddenham, whose father (a Norfolk man) had only recently acquired Tuddenham Manor, presumably because he fancied the name. Her son, also Robert, inherited Wergen Hall and the other holdings, but not Tuddenham which went to his uncle Oliver de Tuddenham, and was promptly disposed of.

This Robert remained as parson at Eriswell where the 1327 Subsidy Return shows he was living in modest comfort. Things improved considerably when his nephew and heir (the clergy were now forbidden to marry) married the niece of Edward I's friend Otto de Grandison, at whose birth, the story goes, an astrologer had predicted he would survive only as long as a piece of coal in the grate. The coal was rescued and carefully kept, enabling Otto not only to live to 100 (when, tired of life, he threw it back into the fire) but also to suck without harm all the poison from a wound of the young Prince (later King) Edward. Part of the resultant rewards came down to enrich the Tuddenhams. Eriswell of course is handy for Cambridge and in 1350 they gave their living of the church in Grundisburgh to St. Michael's House, precursor of Trinity College, the source of many subsequent rectors.

The 1327 Subsidy, a 5 per cent tax on all moveable assets, assessed the taxable value of Grundisburgh cum Burgh at £59 together. In theory everyone was included who had personal property over 5 shillings, half the price of one ox, an endowment many a Domesday freeman would have considered quite meagre; alternatively the equivalent of up to 10 weeks' wages. Out of the villages' combined population probably in excess of a thousand – say two hundred or so households – the Return lists 36 names of whom 19 possessed assets of over £1. One must assume little more than half these figures refer to Grundisburgh: Burgh had the larger population at Domesday (around 400 against 250) but in 1524, when they were assessed separately, there were 31 names under Grundisburgh to Burgh's 22.

For over a century and a half the Tuddenhams were lords of the manor at Grundisburgh. Compared to the fertile and acquisitive Peches, they seem a dull lot. The times were against them. The fourteenth century has much in common with the twentieth: the population explosion of the previous 200 years caused prices, but not at first wages, to double; trade with the continent, vastly increased as a result of the Normans' European connections, created a new class of ultra-rich who didn't hesitate to flaunt their wealth; while the church, conservative and often divided, declined steadily in influence. Materialism produced a crime-wave bordering on anarchy. The two great domestic events of the century, the Black Death in 1349 and the Peasants' Revolt of 1381 (the former killing one-third of the population and the latter following the egalitarian preaching of the new orders of itinerant friars) were more serious and more traumatic than the carnage of the First World War or the social upheaval of the Second. And the peasants' slogan 'A Great Society' has a familiar ring.

By chance the Peasants' Revolt in Suffolk may have been sparked off by the lord of Grundisburgh, great-nephew of Parson Robert and the puissant Otto, John de Tuddenham, who was Sheriff about that time. In January 1381 the Sheriff had received orders to draw up a register for a poll-tax of a shilling a head to comprise the names, addresses and means of everyone over 15. He never thought of calling it the Community Charge and by June looting was widespread led by the self-styled Angels of Satan. It is unlikely that Grundisburgh, as one of the Sheriff's villages, and where at least one person was arrested, remained unharmed. De Tuddenham himself received frequent threats against his life. He survived, however, for another 11 years.

All his children predeceased him, so his estates went to his wife, Margaret, and on to their grandson, Thomas. She married off Thomas at about the age of 12 to an Ashbocking girl called Alice Wodehouse who in middle life had an affair with another man. Thomas obtained a divorce and never remarried, taking up politics instead. Unfortunately he supported the wrong side in the Wars of the Roses and in 1461, now an old man, 5 months after Edward IV had deposed Henry VI, he was beheaded on Tower Hill. Alice went into a Norfolk convent where under her sister-in-law's will she received a small annuity; but by then she must have been a very old lady herself.

This sister of Thomas, Margaret Bedingfield, inherited the Grundisburgh estate and what other pieces of land were not forfeited to the King. The Bedingfields at this period had a knack of spotting the winners and consequently grew more prosperous with every reign. Sigers, as Wergen Hall had become (doubtless named after some long-serving agent or tenant of the Tuddenhams) as a small unit among many larger ones, was possibly more bother than it was worth. Edmund Bedingfield sold it almost as soon as he could after the death of his grandmother Margaret in 1474. Thus ended his family's long association with Grundisburgh, which had continued in unbroken descent from the Norman Conquest.

CHAPTER THREE

Grundisburgh Hall

T H E new owner of Sigers was Sir John Wingfield, head of one of the richest, grandest and largest families in Suffolk. He had 13 children himself, among whose many manors was Thorpe Hall, Hasketon, with land adjoining that of Sigers so that the two might usefully be combined. During the two following generations there is no record of who lived in the house until it was sold around 1550. (The lordship of the manor, however, was dealt with separately, being inherited or purchased in 1589 by Anthony Gosnold of Otley.)

The buyer of Sigers was Katherine Colet, daughter of Thomas Wall who rebuilt Bast's. She was also the sister-in-law of Humphrey Wingfield, and if Sigers had been inherited by him, Katherine's involvement may have been the result of some family rear-rangement. Whatever her plans they never matured, and in 1553 the property was sold again, this time to an elderly merchant from Ipswich called Richard Blois. He paid £400 for the house plus 260 acres, together with Hundlands (a Culpho manor) and three small properties, Goslins Garden, Tanners and Sibbons. Goslins Garden was south of Gull Farm and Sibbons adjoined it. This acreage, which comprised fields scattered over the parish, happens to be of almost similar extent to the Domesday holdings of Hervey de Bourges; not necessarily a coincidence despite the additions and subtractions there must have been in the intervening five centuries.

The Blois family (pronounced to rhyme with voice) for all the Frenchness of their name and the usual hints that they had come over with the Conqueror, were typical of the new middle class of merchants who had risen to affluence under the Tudors. By the standards of the Wingfields, Richard Blois was far from rich: lord of no manor, he would have had the status in Grundisburgh almost comparable to a yeoman farmer. What set him apart was his ability to read and write and the inflation-protection of his business interests.

During the century and a quarter of Tudor rule, prices rose fivefold, the fastest increase before our own times, while wages barely doubled. Grundisburgh was a grim place in those years: the village's taxable value of land and moveables between the Subsidies of 1524 and 1568, a period when values generally doubled, rose 15 per cent to £132. The Subsidy lists are mutilated, and widespread evasion makes them inaccurate anyway, but it is remarkable that only three names appear on both – Heyward, Etheriche and Gildersleeve – out of a total of 31 in 1524 and 21 in 1568. Many men simply found it impossible to make ends meet. They and their wives might take in work from the cloth merchants of Ipswich, or the family might move in the hope of finding better pay elsewhere. Either way – because they had fallen below the tax level or because their houses were empty – they were absent from the Subsidy Returns.

The Blois family had no such problems. At least in the short term, inflation was good for business: fish, dried from Newfoundland or wet from Lowestoft; textiles, exporting honest Suffolk broadcloth to the continent in exchange for silk, saffron and cochineal; sugar from Barbados, plus adding value by refining it in the sugarhouse they built by the quay in Ipswich; wax, soap, lead, they are all mentioned in their account books, the precise compendiums of the family's achievements, which were the centre of their lives. It is clear that Richard and the four Williams who succeeded him, son, grandson, great-grandson and great-great-grandson, loved those ledgers, a curious mélange of business, household and family affairs, often in chatty, diary form about the story of some voyage, marriage or other excitement.

The third William was especially garrulous. Proudly he records how his great-grandfather had bought Sigers 'the largest farm in the village' previously possessed by 'three noble owners' as a house for his retirement and had died there a few years later; how his grandfather had built a new parlour and added a farm called Chamberlains to the domain, plus the village windmill, dating back to the thirteenth century, which he dismantled; and how his father just before his death in 1621 had extended the house further with the latest status-symbol among the better-off, a separate kitchen.

He himself inherited the property while still a young bachelor. An ambitious man, head of a well-established firm, he turned Sigers into a gentleman's residence sporting a grand entrance hall with staircase in the latest (Jacobean) style, and himself into a gentleman. The house was finished just before his marriage in 1624 to Cecily Wingfield, direct descendant of that noble Sir John who had once owned it. This was a social triumph and the perfect excuse to develop an interest in heraldry and genealogy, which he did with gusto. They moved in after a six weeks' honeymoon. By now the name of Sigers had been dropped in favour of the more dignified Grundisburgh Hall.

Some years later he acquired the lordship of the manor from the Gosnolds who, having supported Charles I in the Civil War, may have needed the money; or it may have come to him via Cecily through inheritance. Manors had long since lost their feudal potency, shortage of labour after the Black Death having enabled villagers to commute their obligations for a nominal cash sum and to become copyholders; that is, retain a copy of the manorial record which registered and protected ownership. Lordship was a financial liability, although keeping a measure of prestige (as up to a point it still does) and this no doubt was what William was after.

He now embarked on a programme of selling property in Ipswich and reinvesting the proceeds in land in Grundisburgh, a commuter to town during the week, a country gentleman at weekends. His two largest purchases were a farm named Thornes bought from the Jennors for £1350 and another called Ardelyns previously owned by Robert Sparrow, also an Ipswich merchant (and before him by the Gosnolds) for £684. Price is his only clue to the size of these acquisitions, each of which must have been smaller than the Sigers farm itself. Allowing for inflation and assuming that as an established buyer he paid top prices, justifiable if his capital and modern methods improved returns, it is likely he more than doubled his land in Grundisburgh. 'I desire thankfully to acknowledge', he notes in his accounts, as if congratulating the finance director, 'the goodness of God who was pleased to afford us the opportunity to purchase . . . parcels of land which were either bordering on our lands or else dispersed and scattered among our land which hath made ourselves more complete.'

More exasperating are his oblique clues about the location of his fields: 'the mountain above the house in which we have parcels of Thornes now contains 29 acres . . . the north-east corner (of the mount) contains 13 acres . . . Angel's Bottom on the north side of the brook, 9 acres . . . Hundland's Meadow in which we have 2 acres of Thornes next the mount contains 9 acres . . . Boyton Close by Angel's Gate was most of it Thornes until I added 4 acres called Stoney Pightle (=field) . . . parcels of Angel Field formerly belonging to Thornes . . .'

William and Cecily moved out of Grundisburgh Hall and back to Ipswich in 1651 when their son, the fourth William, got married and took over the estate, including all furniture and outdoor stock, valued and entered in the books at £1200. He married Martha Broke, heiress of Cockfield Hall, Yoxford, and on her death, her widowed sister-in-law, equally wealthy. He, too, as his father records, made some substantial additions to the estate: '4 acres called Bastyes at the bottom of Angel Field he laid into Hundland's Mead . . . now all

Sir Charles Blois, first baronet.

Hundland's Mead contains 22 acres . . . buying Neales and Manns on Hundland Hill . . .'. The total cost was over £7000, much of the land belonging to the two manors of Culpho.

To summarise, it seems that: (i) Hundlands Meadow was near the present entrance to the Grundisburgh Hall domain, stretching north-west towards Culpho; (ii) Hundland Hill went from roughly Pound Corner down towards Culpho; (iii) Angel's Bottom was near Gull Farm at the south-west end of Angel Field; (iv) Angel's Gate was likely to have been on the east side of Angel Field nearest the centre of the village; (v) in which case Stoney Pightle would fit coincidentally beside Stoney Road; (vi) the 4 acres called Bastyes between Hundland's Mead and Angel's Bottom were nowhere near the house now called Bast's; and (vii) the dismantled windmill was probably near the site of the later post-mill, since there are so few better alternatives in the village.

Predeceased by Cecily and six of their eight children, William (No.3) died in 1673, the same age as the century, a meticulous and endearing fusspot; MP under both Cromwell and Charles II, Puritan by conviction, Royalist by sentiment; a sad figure as his hopes apparently faded of founding a great dynasty.

The fourth William, his heir, who outlived him by just two years, had one surviving son, Charles, who inherited his Grundisburgh, Yoxford and other estates. He lived in Grundisburgh until 1693 when, the last of the Broke aunts having died, he was able to move to the more spacious ambience of Cockfield Hall. His first wife had just died and he remarried the following year, so he could make a complete break. At Cockfield he found one last asset included in no will or settlement, a laxative recipe (grass, watercress, liverwort, rhubarb, red dock root, raisins and oranges), which was given to the servants every spring. Even so, his new wife had trouble with them. 'Servants', she said, 'are the greatest plagues on earth.'

Charles made one investment which would surely have pleased his grandfather: in 1686 he bought himself a baronetcy. The price would have been around £2000, £100,000 in today's money, a bargain compared to the £1m. (again in today's money) charged by Lloyd George. Nevertheless it was quite a sum to raise in cash on top of the £9000 he had had to find for his sisters' dowries.

Between 1704 and 1771 Grundisburgh Hall was let. Charles kept a sharp eye on what went on, often taking a party over for dinner, paying a shilling per head. We know the names of the first and last tenants: Robert Warford, a yeoman farmer, who paid £100 a year for the house and garden and Admiral John Byron, the poet's grand-father, who died two years before his grandson was born.

Sir Charles, the first baronet, died in 1738 and was followed in quick succession by numbers two, three, and four. His grandson, number five, 'John Blo', an abbreviation matched by his notable lack of inches, was 21 when he came into the property, and before he was 30 he had gambled away his inheritance. He went abroad to save money (in those far-off days the pound's purchasing power was twice what it was at home) while his assets were sold to pay his creditors. The situation was eased by the demise of one of them, Mr. Fitzgerald, who was soon afterwards hanged for incitement to murder. It was also helped by the foresight of his wife's parents who had got him to settle on her the Blythborough and Yoxford property, including Cockfield, where his descendants flourish to this day.

The Grundisburgh estate was sold in 1772 to a man called Brampton Gurdon Dillingham, the son of a Norfolk landowner. He was born Brampton Gurdon but in 1762 had done a deal with his maternal grandfather, Theophilus Dillingham. At that time Bramp-ton was 22 and wanting to get married, but the old man, on whom he was financially dependent, considered both he and his fiancée were too young. The girl was Mary Bedingfield, a distant cousin of the Edmund Bedingfield who had sold Sigers at the end of the Wars of the Roses. The Gurdons were known for their charm and the young couple soon got round grandfather, who promised to leave them the Dillingham estates on condition his grandson added Dillingham to his name.

Within seven years grandfather and Mary were both dead. Bramp-ton, a widower with three small children – he didn't remarry until 1780 – almost immediately sold the Dillingham property and bought

Grundisburgh Hall with the proceeds, 'a spot', he wrote, 'so very beautiful'. The house was 'old', by which he meant no doubt it had no eighteenth-century improvements, and the estate contained six farms totalling around 900 acres with a rent roll of £771 a year. After a bit of haggling a price of £22,000 was agreed. Roughly 300 acres were in Culpho and the rest in Grundisburgh, the farms for which William Blois had thanked God for His assistance in accumulating.

Brampton had the happy contemporary itch to build. He put an agreeable new front on Grundisburgh Hall, but what he will be remembered for is his commission to John Soane to rebuild Letton, the family home in Norfolk. Soane was a great architect but a very difficult man, so that few chances came his way to build houses for the gentry, and of those, Letton is one of the few surviving. Many were the meetings between client and architect both on site and at Grundisburgh. On one occasion Soane had to buy an umbrella, for which Brampton's account was duly debited with 13 shillings. Despite the rain, Letton was ready by 1787 when Brampton moved in. Was it, after all, a disappointment? After just 9 years he handed it over to his eldest son, Theophilus Thornhagh (pronounced Thorny) Gurdon on his marriage – the Dillingham had been dropped – and returned to Grundisburgh where he died in 1820.

The Hall thereafter was let to General Anson, a distinguished veteran of the Peninsular War, until 1836 when it was briefly occupied by Mary Frere, Brampton's widowed daughter by his second marriage, a lady as widely acclaimed for her singing voice as for her prowess with a gun.

Her step-brother, Thornhagh, was no less formidable. A colonel in the militia (no sinecure during the war when, on Nelson's advice, the coast around Southwold was deemed the likeliest in England for an invasion, and even Grundisburgh was expected to produce 10 army 'volunteers') he never lived in the village, although he was a regular visitor on business as General Anson's guest. During one visit his single-handed pacification of a riot in Tuddenham was favourably compared to the bloodshed caused by the squire of Witnesham who in similar circumstances had called out the local stag hunt. Riots were as endemic during the war and its deflationary aftermath as strikes today, and for the same reasons. Although there was one in Grundisburgh in 1816, there was little trouble otherwise when about that time one-third of the households were receiving some form of poor relief. The men blamed the new threshing machines for their plight: the colonel, who was no monetarist, considered better sanitation and early marriage were the culprits.

His own lifestyle was unaffected by these troubles. There are accounts extant for 1826 which provide an insight into random items

Colonel Theophilus Thornhagh Gurdon.

of expenditure: tailor £148, wines and spirits £173, stables £316, books £5, charities £45. The inflation multiplier for today's equivalent sums is over 40, a total now of £30,000.

The next two generations, Brampton the second and his son Robert, also preferred the Soanesque splendour of Letton, although Brampton did bring up his young family in Grundisburgh from 1840 until his father's death in 1849. Once again, and for the next 40 years, Grundisburgh Hall was let. It was thus available soon after Robert's younger brother William Brampton (Willie to the family, Brampton to everyone else) retired from his job at the Treasury and got married at the age of 45. His career had been brief but distinguished, earning him a knighthood for public services which had included being Gladstone's private secretary. However he and his wife, Camilla, chose married life away from it all in the country; she to edit a book on Suffolk folklore (a subject then vested with inordinate significance) and to write on the theme of Memories and Fancies; he to develop an interest in agriculture, especially pigs.

Priest in the St. Christopher mural.

Bast's.

Green and school, about 1900.

Sir John Blois, fifth and bankrupt baronet.

Grundisburgh Hall, 1787.

Green and old school, 1992.

Brampton Gurdon Dillingham in fancy dress.

This idyllic state lasted five short years when Camilla died aged 36. Sir Brampton left Grundisburgh, reserving two rooms at Elm Tree Farm to enable him to remain on the County Council, and followed his brother Robert into Liberal politics. He gained a seat in Parliament in 1899, soon after Robert, who had disagreed with Gladstone over Irish Home Rule, lost his. Robert accepted a peerage as a consolation, and took the title Cranworth from the village near Letton where many of the family are buried. It is ironic that the Gurdons who for many generations had been an active political family with strong radical inclinations (one is said to have assassinated Richard I, another joined de Montfort's rebellion, a third was a prominent Roundhead) should finally have been ennobled by that arch-Conservative, Lord Salisbury.

Bertram, his son, the second Lord Cranworth, who succeeded in 1902, helped guide the village through the many problems of the twentieth century, popular and respected everywhere, and a firm Conservative. He was a noted raconteur. 'But are your stories all *true*, Lord Cranworth?' asked a brash young man at a Hall tea party. Silence descended. Lady Cranworth froze over the teapot. 'I really can't remember,' he replied affably. He appears in *Akenfield*, in the gardener's story, as Lord Covehithe.

Red Poll cattle, descendants of the hornless Saxon beasts, were his chief agricultural interest, for which he took Elm Tree and Park Farms in hand. Letton was sold during the First World War and Grundisburgh became his home. He died in 1964, aged 86. An iron replica of his garter banner of three leopards' faces was erected on the village green, not only as a memorial to the man but also a reminder that his family still owns the green itself, which the parish leases.

His only son was killed in the Western Desert in the Second World War, so his grandson, Philip, became the third baron, and probably the 37th lord of the manor since the day that Hervey de Bourges rode into the village to help himself.

CHAPTER FOUR

The Church

I SILIA de Bourges, Hervey's daughter, is reputed to be the joint founder of St. Mary's, Grundisburgh. Her partner was Bartholomew de Glanville of Boulge or Alderton. Until the Reformation it would have been known as the church of Our Lady. As Isilia is referred to by her maiden name, the date was around 1100, before her marriage to William Peche. The cost was no doubt incurred by her father and was possibly the penance which, according to the agreeable custom of the time, he would have paid for the lives of the men he had killed at Hastings. No trace of that church remains, except perhaps bits of its foundations under the existing building.

Before that, the people of Grundisburgh along with their neighbours from Burgh had gone to Mass at St. Botolph's chapel, probably no connection with the present church in Burgh which for much of its 700 years has been linked with St. Andrew. This chapel was a place of special pilgrimage since it contained the body of St. Botolph himself, after King Edmund the most charismatic of the early saints, as the many churches dedicated to him testify. He died on June 17th about 675 in his monastery at Iken near Aldeburgh, and his body was moved to Grundisburgh after the Danes' destruction of Iken. No one knows where the chapel was. One theory is a field called Chapel Yard opposite Manor Farm, on the Burgh side of the river and on the path from Grundisburgh's Town Lane. The record's text, however, says Grundisburgh, where now not even a road name commemorates the fact.

The exact site would not matter but for the story of the golden calf. Just before the Conquest, the monks of Bury St. Edmunds, relying on some old permission of King Canute, decided to steal St. Botolph's bones (the incident is related by another Bury monk about a generation later) in order to increase the attractions of their own monastery as a place of pilgrimage. They chose a dark night, somehow convincing themselves that the thunderstorm that attended their pillage was a sign of divine approval. They left behind the chapel's main adornment, a curious votive offering even for Saxon

Suffolk where paganism was still just below the surface, the golden statue of a calf. The villagers, no doubt fearing for its safety now that St. Botolph had deserted them, buried the statue outside the chapel where, according to legend, it remains to this day. St. Botolph, for his part, is likely to have been finally laid to rest, cremated in the great fire at Bury Abbey in 1465.

It was Hugh Peche, Isilia's great-great-grandson, who built the earliest part of the present St. Mary's. From the dog-tooth decoration of the piscina in the chancel to the right of the altar, this can be dated to about 1280. The three walls of the chancel itself are all that remain of Hugh's efforts, the north and south windows having been modernised about 100 years later, and the east window in 1872. The whole church, whose length included at least one-third of the present nave, dark and intimate to suit the mood of the time, would have slightly resembled the church at Culpho.

The advowson or patronage of Isilia's church was held by the Abbot of Ely, some slender indication that it had been built as a penance. Hugh, after a bit of unpleasantness, kept it for himself. Apart from the prestige, this afforded him a degree of financial flexibility. Although tithes were compulsory on all free men, the patron of a living was allowed to devote two-thirds of the tithes payable by himself to any religious charity he liked. This could obviously be convenient in all sorts of ways, including the provision of donations to the charity which begins at home.

St. Mary's first Rector of whom there is record was a contemporary of Hugh's called Ralph de Blumville. Whether he ever ministered, or even lived, in the parish, is another matter. It was common practice in those days, when many of the clergy spoke only French, to appoint a 'Mass-priest', often one of the villagers who hopefully could read, to get through the basic worship of the church (more like a modern worker-priest than the curate we are accustomed to) while the Rector collected and spent the tithes. Several Rectors in the following century do not sound like local men: Jacobus de Krek, William del Sonn Capellanus and Cardinal Alonconis, also Archdeacon of Suffolk, who never came to England, let alone Grundisburgh, at all.

During the fourteenth century under the Tuddenhams, the nave was rebuilt and lengthened to its present size and the south aisle added. Not only had the population been increasing but there was a reaction, as there is today, away from the old mumbled Mass to a brighter church with a more active ritual for which space was needed. On the south wall of the chancel (removed thither from the nave's north wall in 1961) is a fragment of a mural, a few simple lines of remarkable power, said to be of St. Margaret, the patron saint not

St. Margaret (from the mural in St. Mary's chancel).

only of the peasants but also of Margaret de Tuddenham, wife of the Sheriff during the Peasants' Revolt; a gesture possibly of reconciliation between Them and Us, and a reminder, certainly, of who was paying.

Among the work of those years would have been the erection of the church tower, doubling up as a porch, like the present one which replaced it. Its main purpose, of course, was as a belfry, the beginning of that custom of ringing bells whose sound is so uniquely evocative of the Middle Ages. That is slightly deceptive in St. Mary's case, since today's elaborate change-ringing of its twelve bells (a couple were added for the Diamond Jubilee, a couple more in 1949 and another pair in 1990) must be a far cry indeed from the simple sounds of the fourteenth century.

We have no clue about how Grundisburgh was affected by the Black Death. Some villages, for example Barchester down the road, were wiped out altogether. There is a theory that this part of Suffolk did not suffer too badly, but the fact remains that throughout the county, deaths among the clergy in 1349 were ten times the annual average of the previous five years. (Grundisburgh's Rector, Walter de Wancey, survived, but he may have been non-resident.) Moreover the Black Death was merely the first and worst of a series of plagues to hit the area over the following century.

That happens to be the period which produced the two outstanding features of St. Mary's, the clerestory and the double hammer-beam roof, which as everybody knows is among the finest in Suffolk. On the outside south wall of the clerestory, beside the arms of the Tuddenhams, are the initials T and A, most likely those of Thomas and Alice who were divorced in 1436. If so, the clerestory obviously pre-dates the divorce, but the roof may have been a little later. Was it built by Margaret Bedingfield, Thomas's sister, a woman of great piety, as a memorial to her brother after his execution, its fifty hovering angels carrying his soul to Heaven? And whose face was the priest's (surely taken from the life) fishing in the river in the giant mural of St. Christopher on the church's north wall?

Although their names are recorded, we know as little about the thirty-eight Rectors of the present St. Mary's as we do about most of the 10,000 or more souls who have lived during the past 700 years under their care. The most intriguing is Edward Marr whose ministry spanned the whole Reformation, Henry VIII's break with Rome, Mary's reunion, and the Elizabethan settlement. He seems to have taken these complexities in his stride, like most of his parishioners who, now that they could read or hear the Bible in English, were beginning, as Sir Thomas More had feared, to think for themselves. Indeed, compared to the liturgical changes of our own day, they had little to complain about.

Was it the Rector who warned Alice Driver, Grundisburgh's Protestant martyr, that the authorities were after her? She and a friend from Woodbridge hid in a hay loft near her home where they were found and taken off to Melton jail. She was a ploughman's daughter, 30 years old, married but childless, and educated as she made clear at her trial, only in the university of life. She was burned at the stake in Cornhill, Ipswich, in November 1558, just a fortnight before the death of Bloody Mary, which would have saved her life. The fate of her husband, who seems to have kept a low profile throughout, is not known.

Under Elizabeth, Catholics in turn were hit hard, but usually, and more effectively, in their pockets, fined up to £20 a month for non-attendance at church, £50,000 a year today. Two were prominent in Grundisburgh, Anne Mannock and her son-in-law, Thomas Sulyard, a Bedingfield on his mother's side, who served time in Framlingham jail, no doubt having run out of money. In spite of everything, they were both buried in St. Mary's, still praying there perhaps for better days.

Father (or Mr.) Marr's hand is also detectable in the delicate matter of the village guild. This had been started probably before the Black

Death to arrange Masses for the souls of former members (which, as it still does, costs money) and to help the sick and needy. It also organised Church Ales, the equivalent of a modern bazaar, but more frequent, more profitable and much more rowdy: half a dozen a year, raising £20 a time, was not uncommon. It was a fraternity like the craft guilds of the towns, open to everybody, men and women, on payment of a small subscription like a halfpenny. Over the years its assets had built up thanks to gifts and legacies (the largest was from John Yate, a priest in Burgh) and in the Subsidy Returns of 1524, the Grundisburgh guild is shown with rents of £4 a year. In 1545 Parliament vested in the Crown the property of all guilds unless they were totally non-religious. Somehow Grundisburgh's survived, resurfacing in the 1568 Subsidy as Town Lands.

Somehow, also, the church's fine fourteenth-century rood screen survived, Edward Marr's enduring memorial. On explicit instructions from his superiors it had to go. One imagines it was dismantled and stored in some Parsonage barn, awaiting conversion, if anyone asked, into seats or bedsteads, the ignominious fate of so many others that escaped the bonfires. At about the same time the stairs to the gallery above the screen would have been blocked off and the church walls whitewashed to efface Saints Christopher, Margaret and the other paintings.

Puritanism in the next century flourished in East Anglia as nowhere else in England, and there can be little doubt that from the Bloises downwards most people in Grundisburgh during the Civil War were on the side of Parliament against the King. The main exception was the Rector, Edward Barton, on whom the main burden of the new dispensation inevitably fell, the greatest upheaval St. Mary's had known since the six years in King John's reign when services throughout the country had been suspended by Papal interdict.

He was a sick man in his late thirties when he came to the village in 1640 with a weak voice, disastrous in an age which enjoyed sermons. He limited himself to half an hour, and having been ejected for idleness in 1644 by the Suffolk Committee for the Trial of Scandalous Ministers, died within the year. William Blois, the third, was a member of this committee, and so by a coincidence was Colonel Brampton Gurdon, the family's first recorded connection with the village.

Mr. Barton's successor, Richard Jennings, who had emigrated to New England and then thought better of it, lasted an even shorter time. He was followed by Richard Culverwell, a member of a distinguished Puritan family and, although he was too late to save the angels' heads in the roof, it was probably thanks to his authority

Colonel Brampton Gurdon, the Roundhead.

that the vandalism, which damaged chiefly the pew-ends, the font and the stained glass was no worse. A few pieces of glass survive, out of easy reach at the top of some of the windows.

Another exception to the Puritan mood was the tenant or owner of Bast's, possibly William Thinge, Robert's grandfather, who is supposed to have harboured 200 Royalist troops in his attic, hence the improbable legend that this is why the south-west end of the house leans outwards.

The Puritanism of the Bloises did not prevent the last two Williams adorning the north wall of the chancel with funeral plaques, the central one chiefly in memory of the aristocratic Cecily with a long heraldic inscription composed unmistakably by her husband (costing as he records £33); while to its left is another for her daughter-in-law, Martha, complete with her profile in low relief, first wife of the fourth William and the prime cause of the family's removal to Cockfield. On the right, a pompous display encloses the epitaph of their son Charles, the first baronet.

About this time, probably soon after new bells were hoisted in 1665, the church's old flint tower began to crumble. The reason could well have been the installation of a three-quarters wheel for hanging the bells, an important technical innovation which greatly

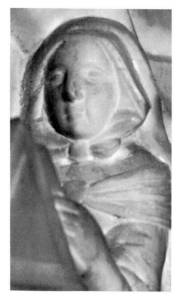

Martha Blois. (From the
funeral plaque in St. Mary's
chancel.)

William Blois, the fourth,
her husband.

increased the vibrations. The bells were stored at the back of the
church but nothing was done for about 60 years until money for
another tower was forthcoming under the will of Robert Thinge
from the sale of his property in Hasketon.

Robert was a bachelor, for many years a churchwarden, who
reinvested his inheritance from the family grocery business into real
estate, which like William Blois, enabled him to call himself a
gentleman. He stipulated the new 'steeple' or tower should be of
brick, hopefully thinking of Suffolk white brick, then a fashionable
substitute, as it was imagined, for stone. Red brick was what he got,
no doubt cheaper, which may have been important; and which, as it
turned out, harmonises better with the regulation materials used in
later years on the Victorian school next door. 'Life pass like a
Shadow', says the inscription above the tower's sundial. Was that an
expression Robert in his Suffolk accent was apt to quote? Or is there
simply an apostrophe missing?

The new tower must have contrasted strangely with the decaying
fabric of the rest of the church, which the faithful continued for a
further 150 years to patch up with the crudest expedients. Many of
course were not interested, practising what was known as horse-
religion, working for six days, sleeping on the seventh.

A visitor on a Sunday in 1858 noted the church was less than half
full and that the new box pews were so deep it was impossible, when

Mr. Hakewill's drawing for his proposed spire of St. Mary's.

sitting down, to see the Rector at the lectern, while the chancel pews
were actually facing the wrong way (like the pews still at Ramsholt)
with their backs to the altar. There was a high oak pulpit half-way
down the north wall of the nave, whence George Webster, Rector
between 1832 and 1870, one of the longest incumbencies, would
deliver his sermons in a voice ranging with random emphasis from
screech to whisper which made comprehension extremely hard.

He was followed by Henry Turner, who at once began the radical
restoration work that was to continue off and on for twenty years.
Mr. E.C. Hakewill was hired, the romantic architect of Playford
Mount, built for his own retirement. St. Mary's, he reported, was
the victim of cold neglect and bad taste.

The box pews were swept away, the organ loft at the back of the
church, encrusted with Holy Writ, dismantled, and the east and west
windows enlarged to their original dimensions. The old font,
supported by its poodle-like lions (but who in fifteenth-century
Grundisburgh had ever seen a lion?) was given a new base at the
architect's personal expense. The elegant Lady Chapel which had
been rebuilt in 1527 by Thomas Wall in memory of his parents and
the family salt business (an unscanned and ill-rhymed doggerel
records the fact in memorial brass) was reincorporated into the

church by the removal of a high brick partition. It remained the vestry: neither Rector nor congregation felt themselves High Church enough to restore its original use. And after over two centuries the angels got their heads back, plus new wings free of woodworm.

Death intervened before Mr. Hakewill could realise his ambition to reface Robert Thinge's tower with flint and crown it with a spire, perhaps under the impression that this was what was intended by the word 'steeple' in his will. In his gothick exuberance, the architect never had time or money to repair the church's flintwork, or to address himself to the problem that St. Mary's had become a stage set, to be viewed from one side only, the south. The result is the stucco surface of the outer walls today, the flint of the clerestory alone showing what might have been.

In the midst of the church restoration, the opportunity was taken to rebuild the moated medieval Rectory in a sort of Tudor style, happily the only house of its kind in Suffolk to be designed by H.A. Darbyshire, and a monument to the affluence of the Rector. In 1840 his income including tithes was £1000 a year, 50 times the basic agricultural wage. In 1291, it had been £17 or about 14 times the basic wage. It was still £17 in 1535 on the eve of the Reformation, a decline in purchasing power of nearly two-thirds. Even so, the differential looks higher than it is today.

The Victorian pendulum had swung too far, and the tithe system, almost untouched since it was tidied up by the Normans, was the obvious candidate for reform. The intention was to reduce the burden at once by a small amount, and in the longer term to make it more responsive to economic conditions and official control. Tithes, the church's 10 per cent tax on labour, livestock and the fruits of the earth, had always been unpopular: payable in kind, rigidly enforced and tempting to evade, the exact amount due was at best an annual niggle and at worst, in bad times, a grievous imposition. Thomas Kechin, Edward Barton's predecessor in Grundisburgh, had felt compelled to sue his parishioners for £40 underpayment, not an act to endear a shepherd to his flock, and it is most unlikely this was the village's only case. (That was just one of Mr. Kechin's financial problems: another was the discovery that his curate, Pitman, was an undischarged bankrupt.)

The vicious deflation after Waterloo and the idea that tithes were discouraging agricultural innovation, not to mention the growth of non-conformism, brought matters to a head, and in the Act of 1836 tithes were commuted for annual cash payments linked to an index of cereal prices.

Grundisburgh's tithes were commuted in 1842 for £543 a year. Like those everywhere else, they had been governed by a set of local

Mr. H.A. Darbyshire's Rectory (now the Old Rectory).

customs, generations old, laboriously copied out afresh, sometimes amended, for every new Rector. They read like instructions in a game of Monopoly. Already by 1706 – the earliest extant copy – cash alternatives were available on some items: a hearth hen (that is, a hen payable by every titheable household) in lieu of wood or 8 pence; 6 pence for a cow and calf if less than 7 (also payable by every household that had one, as many did until very recently); from farms, 1 calf out of 10 at 5 weeks old or 10 shillings, but for 7 calves or less, deduct 4½ pence; a shilling for every colt foaled; 1 lamb out of 7 or 2 out of 17; pigs ditto when a month old or half-a-crown (30 pence); 1 goose if 7; 2 eggs per hen (later altered to the more evasive 'eggs at Eastertide'); 80 pence per acre of hops (increased by 1834 to 10 shillings: in Kent it was often 50 shillings); 3 or 4 pence per acre for the labour of mowing meadows. 'Tithe corn, hemp, flax, fruit and wool payable in kind . . . no tithe on hay, milk or cheese.' Hemp had been an important and highly profitable crop in Grundisburgh since the fourteenth century; in 1342 its tithe of 160 pence has been estimated as the largest item on the list.

The actual tithe apportionment among the parishioners together with its accompanying map (26.7 inches to the mile) has left us an outstanding snapshot of 1842, a record second only to Domesday itself. Once again taxation was its origin, the great catalyst ensuring a degree of accuracy through a balance of conflicting interests. And it coincides with the first detailed census of the village, a remarkable stroke of luck for the historian.

The glebe land of 47 acres, let in a dozen separate parcels, was assessed at nil, a fact which may have been reflected in a higher rent charge. Robert Ablitt of Wood Farm, a Baptist, also escaped virtually scot-free as a result of a shrewd modus or private commutation for a lump sum negotiated about thirty years earlier. About 60 households out of 175 were assessed for payment, nearly half the total being found by three families, the Harrises, the Manbys and the Catts. The latter were based at Clopton Hall but also had White-house Farm and other land in Grundisburgh. The Gurdons had no farms in hand and their tithes were just 26 shillings. No farm, cottage or house is mentioned by name, only the 400 or so fields, of which remarkably few are identifiable today, and none at all with those mentioned in the seventeenth century by William Blois in his account books. Farmers no doubt were often pressed by the tithe commissioners for names and provided some off the tops of their heads. At that date about 20 per cent of the parish was meadowland compared to under 5 per cent both now and at the time of Domesday.

By 1936, thanks to the productivity of the North American prairies, Grundisburgh's tithes had fallen nearly 25 per cent to £421, and Parliament decided that, having thrown out the bathwater a century earlier, it was time for the baby to go as well. With monumental mistiming, tithes were abolished in exchange for an annuity payable in one lump or on easy terms over 60 years, the cash received being largely invested in fixed interest stock. Glebe lands were likewise gradually disposed of and their proceeds suffered a similar fate. Grundisburgh's by 1953 were down to 19 acres and by 1991 to about 4. The Rectory itself was sold in 1981. Its old castellated stables (now Ford House) described by a planning officer as 'a rewarding little cornerpiece', which had survived Mr. Darby-shire's pencil, might have made a suitable new Rectory, but a modern house was chosen ½ mile from the church at the end of a quiet lane off the Woodbridge Road. Parishioners apparently wanted a more private location to visit their Rector.

CHAPTER FIVE

The Chapel

GRUNDISBURGH'S history reveals no man more remarkable, nor one whose personality had a greater impact on village life, than John Thompson, the founder of the Baptist chapel, and for 28 years its Pastor.

His parents, who were tenant farmers of the 140 acres of Culpho Hall and owned two smaller properties in Playford and Great Bealings, were devout members of the Church of England, as he was himself until his early 20s when a chance conversation with a Baptist shoemaker 'in his neighbourhood' (one of the multitude in Grundisburgh?) set him thinking. He married a girl called Lucy who, if she didn't share his religious inclinations, must have been astonishingly adaptable.

Finally, in his 26th year, after much loss of sleep and appetite, he literally took the plunge and was received into the Baptist church.

Chapel Outing, about 1905. (The clock says 6.30.)

Baptism at Culpho.

Nothing is recorded about Lucy. Both sets of parents were aghast, and terrible family rows ensued until, during one of them, he was inspired to quote from the Psalms 'when my mother and my father forsake me, then the Lord will take me up'. No medieval miracle could have produced a more gratifying effect: his mother burst into tears and promised she would never forsake him, while the others who were present – father, in-laws and servants – were soon all sobbing away with her. Thereafter it was plain sailing, although his friends, who were made of sterner stuff, never forgave him.

Although he later called himself an agriculturalist, Thompson (living with Lucy on one of his father's farms) seems at this period to have been less interested in farming, having set up as a merchant and dealer. That may have appeared a quicker way to riches, and the wherewithal to spread the Gospel; or it may have fitted in better with his church activities.

One day he was invited to preach in Grundisburgh by Stephen Lawrence who had a smallholding near the top of the track, now Meeting Lane, which led up from the green through the fields towards the post-mill. For about a year Stephen had held Baptist meetings at his home presided over by 'a Mr. George' of Woodbridge (whom curiously Thompson seems to know nothing about) which were at first so successful that a little chapel was added to the house. Perhaps its less cosy atmosphere didn't suit Mr. George's fireside style, and the congregation almost immediately melted away.

Thompson first preached in Grundisburgh in 1797. Within weeks the chapel was overflowing and by July the following year he had taken over the Lawrences' lease, knocked down their house, replaced the little chapel with the present one (to seat 800) and formed the Grundisburgh church of Particular Calvinistic Baptists with a membership of 45 and himself as Pastor. He paid for everything out of his own pocket, even acquiring, or building, six cottages nearby and a house which was divided into three dwellings, in one of which he settled Brother J. Pooley, surely a descendant of the Cromwellian Christopher Pooley, a founding father of the Suffolk Baptists. Nothing more is heard of Brother Lawrence.

It would be fascinating to have examples of the oratorical spell with which every Sunday, morning, afternoon and evening, he was able to bind nearly a thousand people, most of whom had come from surrounding villages to spend the day in Grundisburgh, stern, serious folk, we are told – the men side-whiskered but otherwise clean-shaven – who between services must have overflowed in their hundreds onto the green and everywhere else. We only know that his style was humourless and deeply earnest, something one might have guessed from one of his few remarks that have come down to us, that 'he was unconscious of having committed more than three or four sins in the course of his life'.

It was this sort of remark as well as their aggressive search for converts, not to mention the 'humble walk', which made the Baptists so unpopular, 'pograms', as they were nicknamed, a local variant of the contemporary slang 'fogram', or in modern usage, 'fogey'. In his first eleven years in Grundisburgh, Thompson's baptisms averaged nearly one a week, in a pool in the river at Culpho near Playford bridge. Brampton Dillingham, the landlord of Culpho Hall, was much criticised in certain quarters for permitting such goings-on.

It is clear from the registers and memorials in the burial ground beside the chapel that a great many village families were involved: Ablitt and Harris, the farmers, Cotton, Dunnett, Graystone, Hazelwood, Tye and Woolnough plus many of the very poorest families whose children were given first names like Aaron, Isaac and Ebenezer. This stream of defections from the established church must have been a factor in the 'cold neglect' of St. Mary's during the nineteenth century. By 1825, roughly one-third of the households in the village were Baptists.

Conversions came from careful staff-work as well as preaching. In 1810 Thompson apparently timed a campaign in Wickham Market to coincide with the temporary absence of the Vicar. It slightly backfired when, for three exciting months of Sundays, members of the vestry and several hundred supporters, with no parson to control them, took up the challenge with stones, rotten eggs and other unsavoury missiles as well as fireworks and a large Indian gong. Some windows were broken and a fire started, but as no one seems to have been badly hurt and many of their assailants were (in the Baptist phrase) disguised in liquor, it sounds a bit much to call it, as they did, a persecution. Thompson's reputation, however, was greatly enhanced.

Tithes naturally rankled (Culpho Hall's had been commuted for a lump sum) as did taxes generally, and the brethren were wont to debate whether it was morally right to evade them. Thompson himself was nearly arrested by the excise authorities, who briefly seized the chapel as security. That may have been connected with the financial disaster which overwhelmed his business activities in 1815. It is possible that like many others he was wrong-footed by the outcome of the Battle of Waterloo and the ending of the war. Whatever the reason, he was declared bankrupt and all the property inherited from his father plus his quarter share of the brig *Venus*, 145 tons, and the chapel and cottages in Grundisburgh, were sold to pay his debts. Mr. Dillingham allowed him to retain the lease of Culpho Hall, but the stock was sold. The chapel which, with the additions of the Sunday schoolroom and scullery on its south side, had cost him £1,000, was knocked down at auction for £580.

Thompson's usual vitality and cheerfulness temporarily deserted him. On the Sunday after the sale he preached at Tuddenham on the text 'we wept as we remembered Zion', working himself, and no doubt the congregation, into a state of tearful despair. Next week however he was back at Grundisburgh, Zion restored to him, its copyhold secured in trustees' names on a £300 mortgage.

He died in 1826 and was succeeded by a former draper's assistant from Northamptonshire called Samuel Collins who remained Pastor for 49 years. His first sermon was a memorable one, not so much because of its content but because he preached it every year, with two remissions, on the anniversary of the chapel's foundation. A stout, fatherly figure, at least in middle age, he lacked in his preaching style the nervous energy of his predecessor and it was grimly likened to the rambling structure of a Suffolk farmhouse with

The Chapel.

great oak beams in every room. At a time when some Suffolk congregations were becoming more indulgent in their observances, he kept Grundisburgh on the strict path of its founder, supported by Thompson's youngest son, James, one of his deacons, who had taken on the lease of Culpho Hall after his father's death.

Missionary work was Sam Collins's first love, both as editor of the *Gospel Herald* and organiser of his brain-child the Home Missionary Society, a time-consuming activity. Despite, or because of, all this, membership began to decline. When he arrived it had been over 350: by 1878 it was 229 of which about a quarter were from Grundisburgh.

He was followed by William Dexter, the son of a Jamaican missionary, in a pastorate of just four years. During that time the baptistery was installed beneath the large hinged platform at the front of the chapel, an oval bath some 18 inches deep which had to be filled by buckets from a pump outside. No longer after lunch was it necessary for the church to 'adjourn to the water' of the River Fynn, the congregation usually hundreds strong, the Pastor in his rubberised boiler-suit, the baptismal candidates in their white robes. Now it could all happen within the bare walls of the chapel itself, pastel-dappled from the windows' stained glass, the schoolroom stove only a few damp feet away; and the next morning the white robes would flutter from a clothes-line beside the burial ground.

The great days were over. Grundisburgh was no longer the plum it had once been, and in the fifty years following Mr. Dexter's resignation, the chapel got through seven pastors. Membership was around 150 when Sir Brampton Gurdon retired to Grundisburgh Hall in the 1880s. We are told he was a regular Baptist worshipper. That does not mean he was a baptised member. He remained a

Samuel Collins.

communicant of the Church of England and was buried beside his wife in St. Mary's churchyard.

The chapel's bicentenary is approaching. The fabric is showing its age, the scrubbed pine of the original box-pews has given way to varnished benches, but otherwise little has changed. What would Thompson say now about their empty spaces?

CHAPTER SIX

_____ ❦ _____

The Victorian Censuses

S UDDENLY, with the census of 1841, the fog of history is lightened by a pale sunburst of information, moving pictures in place of the faded still photographs from wills, church records and manorial rolls.

The 1674 Hearth Tax had provided the first complete list of every householder whether he or she was liable to the tax or not, and from this it is clear that Grundisburgh's population then was no more than 300, compared to about 250 at Domesday. During the intervening period, the numbers, having perhaps doubled until the Black Death, collapsed thereafter and probably continued to decline gently over the next 300 years, more a result of economic than physical ailments. It has been estimated that for forty years after 1674 the population in this part of Suffolk fell by around 15 per cent, so that (if correct) there were no more people in Grundisburgh in 1715 than at the time of Domesday.

Thenceforward the incremental prosperity enjoyed for over a century by the occupants of the Hall and the Rectory began to filter down to the villagers themselves, helped to some degree by a nationwide decline in the mortality rate. The census of 1801, the first of the series which has enlivened us all every tenth year since, records a population of 641, a 2½-fold increase on the supposedly low point of 1715.

Happily the bureaucrats soon warmed to their new tool, and by 1841 when the total of 874 showed the remarkable growth-rate was continuing, the requirements of name, age and occupation were added to the simple head-count. All this, combined with the coincidence of the 1842 Tithe Apportionment map plus in 1851 the addition of place of birth, makes it possible to fit together a recognisable jig-saw, even though some pieces are missing and some ambiguous. The assumption is that, short of any contrary indication, consecutive numbers on the census forms denote neighbouring houses; but subsequent divisions and alterations are liable to make precise addresses uncertain.

South side of green about 1920.

The census was not concerned with relationships between households (which would require a separate study embracing the whole
district); and, apart from the same surname, the same Christian
names were shared by many families, which, with the exception of
some of the poorest Baptists, recur with confusing frequency: John,
William and James; Mary, Ann, Sarah and Elizabeth (not an Albert
among them and only one Victoria). Some parents, who had lost one
child in infancy, gave the same name to another a few years later.
Birthplaces are thus helpful in sorting out their comings and goings.
Almost everyone had relations in neighbouring parishes, and it was
no big deal to move to or from one of them. Only seven surnames in
the Hearth Tax list of 1674 recur in the 1841 census (Blowers, Cage,
Cook, Cutting, Oxborrow, Reynolds and Tye) and obviously some
or all could be coincidental. Burch, on the other hand, still a
prominent village family, as well as Cotton, Crapnell, Hart and
Nunn, whose names occur in no taxation list, appear in the parish
register as early as the sixteenth century. One can see the details of
this process continuing through the Victorian censuses; and children
who typically appear in one census only, having been born and flown
the nest within the twenty-year span (Life pass like a Shadow) often
fail to appear in the next as householders in their own right, or
married to householders.

By 1841 the population of Grundisburgh would have almost
doubled in the lifetime of the older inhabitants: more bustle, more
building even than today, more hens, cows and children everywhere;
the noise of more carts on unmetalled roads, the noise of the two
forges on the village green.

Jonathan Groom, the blacksmith at the larger forge (now Forge
House) on the south-west corner of the green, died in 1845. William,

presumably his younger brother and partner, who lived opposite and had recently lost his 14-year-old only daughter, was unable or unwilling to continue the business. His wife Sarah became the only breadwinner, teaching (as she had for some years) at the parochial school, now the Parish Rooms. Meanwhile John Crapnell and his young family moved from Clopton to become the blacksmith.

The other blacksmith in 1841 was Jeremiah Motum, whose forge was on the present site of Oakenfull's Stores. Twenty-year-old Susan Motum (his twin?) looked after him, soon to be replaced by another Susan, Miss Cresswell from the Post Office, whom he married in 1845.

Across the green, in what is now the Williams' shop, was the main village store, a grocer's and draper's, run by Edward and Elizabeth Braham with one assistant and a pair of daughters, all three of their sons being dead.

Beyond Forge House was the chief butcher's shop owned by another Groom, Joseph, a bachelor, with an elderly maid-servant as housekeeper. He married into the Newson farming family and around 1848 moved to Whitehouse Farm, leaving a tenant or manager in the shop, James Banyard.

The present Post Office was originally a cottage – one of several on the site – which was taken over during the 1840s by James Garnham as another grocer's and draper's shop. Next door at Brooklands (it is simpler to use modern names) were Sarah and James Parker, a bricklayer employing two men. He had previously lived with his mother, Maria, and his sisters and a vet presumably the lodger, in Red Cottage on the other side of the Driftway (later called Maltings Lane). Maria owned both Red Cottage and the adjoining Daisy Cottage, keeping the latter as an ale-house which had been started by her late husband, himself a bricklayer, called the Bricklayer's Arms. Stretching behind both houses he had built a small maltings.

Two doors up at Red House were Sarah and Sam Collins, the Baptist Pastor, with their children, Zipporah, Hephzibah, Samuel, Ebenezer, Ruth, Catherine, Frederick and Robert. Beyond them lived the postmistress Maria Cresswell, described – it was before Trollope had introduced the French pillar box – as 'tailor and letter receiver'.

On the other side of Rose Hill, the two main houses were occupied by doctors (strictly they were surgeons and so called themselves 'Mr.', but they acted as G.P.s): Edward Acton at Greenbank and William Steggall at The Chestnuts. William died in 1851: the Steggalls moved out, and the Meggalls with their dame school moved in.

Half Moon and customers. (Mrs. Richardson at the window.)

At what is still called The Old Bakery, the Forsdicks had their baker's shop. After old John Forsdick's death in the 1840s, it was taken on by George and Harriet. George may originally have been a shoemaker, of which there were at least eight in Grundisburgh – a reminder of how much people walked – with two of them in prime locations only a few yards from the bakery: James Woolnough just the other side of Meeting Lane and John Graystone next to the Dog.

Such were the people round the centre of Grundisburgh in the 1840s who had contributed the most and gained the most from the village's great expansion. The Half Moon inn on the Woodbridge Road was another focal point. Here Sarah Ablitt had a grocer's shop, probably in Thatched Cottage. In and around Half Moon Lane there were four families of Smith, two of whom were shoemakers, with two more shoemakers round the corner.

Between them all they provided everything that was needed from day to day. Their custom must have come in part from surrounding villages: it is difficult to believe Grundisburgh alone could have kept three or four butchers in business, let alone all those shoemakers. The market gardens – three of them off Lower Road – were the greengrocers, and old Fanny Frost who lived up Stoney Road sold fruit, no doubt from a barrow. There was a rat-catcher, Jeremiah Dammant (his son Isaac was another shoemaker) and a chimney sweep, Isaac Lovell, and a couple of thatchers, the Leeches, who dwelt up in the sticks beyond Poplar Farm. There was also a seedsman called Noah Thrower. The poor and the rich – the farm workers and their employers – require a separate chapter.

The railway came to Bealings in June 1859. Grundisburgh was jerked into the great world. Timetables and the electric telegraph rendered obsolete overnight the sundial on the church tower and all that it represented. People with new ideas arrived from remote places like London and Salisbury, while many others, especially during the agricultural depression of the 1870s, left for the shorter hours and higher pay of the towns. In 1841, 68 householders out of a total of 175 were farm labourers: in 1881 it was 49 out of 184. The proportion of children under 13 in the village fell over the same period from nearly one-third to under a quarter. New jobs – engine driver, photographer, policeman, charwoman – are recorded. And overall, Grundisburgh's population which had shrunk slightly during the 1840s to 801, declined slowly for a century thereafter.

Edward Braham, the grocer-draper on the village green, died in the winter of 1859. James Garnham moved down the hill to take on the shop. There was a new grocer and draper on Rose Hill, Hester and John Cobb, adjoining Banyard's butcher's shop.

After James's death (when Mrs Garnham got a job at the Melton asylum) Hester Cobb, now a widow with four children, did exactly what they had done and moved down the hill to take charge of the larger shop. She was soon replaced by Arthur Savage, a 30-year-old bachelor with a brother of eight. He was also the postmaster. Maria Cresswell had died in 1863 and her assistant, James Clarke, master tailor, had moved with the Post Office to Joseph Moye's old tailor's shop on the green next to Woolnough the shoemaker. In 1880 he passed on the post business to Arthur Savage.

Ettie Dunnett, 25 in 1881, was the grocer and draper in the Cobbs' old shop on Rose Hill. She was Joseph Dunnett's daughter who also had a grocer's shop. He and his wife when they were first married had lodged with her uncle, William Flory, in one of his five houses in Lower Road (Rosemaree Cottage and others nearby). Dunnett, like Flory, was originally a woodman. His grocer's shop is now The Firs. By the 1880s, Dunnett and Savage were the village's main grocers, and during her brief tenure as mistress of the Hall, Lady Camilla Gurdon placed her orders with each of them in alternate weeks.

Ettie's neighbour at the butcher's shop was no longer James Banyard, who had at last got married and moved away. The new butcher was Frederick Groom, son of the Joseph Groom who had lived and worked there around 1840 before his marriage.

Her neighbours on the other side at Sydney (now Portland) House were Fanny and James Pottle, a landscape gardener employed at the Hall. Fanny (Mrs. Bottle) had a drink problem which soon killed her and she is said to haunt the place. It was the Pottles who installed the greenhouse, the hothouse, the vinery, the rose awning, the mushroom shed and the cucumber pit mentioned in the sale particulars

Basketmaker's Cottage and members of the Pipe family.

when the property was bought about 1886 by Ettie's cousin 'Gentleman' John Dunnett, the coal merchant.

Going back to 1861, the Bricklayer's Arms was no more, its closure roughly coinciding with the arrival of Grundisburgh's first policeman, the hopefully well-named P.C. Friend who lived in the Driftway. Likewise his removal a few years later to the top of Rose Hill may have been the signal for Mileson Mallett, a poulterer and clothes dealer, to diversify into beer and open the Barley Mow at Brooklands.

Three doors up the hill, Hillingdon was bought by Henry Manby of Bast's for his future retirement. He also acquired Daisy Cottage, no doubt to be able to control who lived next door, remembering its history as an ale-house. In 1871 Red Cottage was occupied by Mary Dennington, (former maid-servant of Mrs. Robinson the schoolmistress at Bridge House), who must have lied or been mistaken about her age – an exceptional jump from 30 to 56 in ten years – and was now her heiress; she was also her niece, which was not mentioned to the Census enumerator. A certain latitude was not infrequently taken with ages: women typically going from 25 to 40 in ten years and men from 35 to 50: the greater the age presumably, the greater the truth.

Among the newcomers at the top of the hill in 1871 were Henry Wright, the relieving officer of the Nacton workhouse at Laurel Cottage and Henry Groom, carpenter and parish clerk. He had come from Ivy Cottage (now the Coach House car park) where his father, the tireless Herman, had sired some or all of his 18 children.

At The Chestnuts opposite, the Meggalls had moved out by 1861 and the Steggalls returned, old Dr William's four unmarried children: Rebecca who carried on with Mrs. Meggall's school, John, a male midwife, Mary who kept house, and Charles the eldest who did nothing. Mrs. Acton, just widowed, remained for a time at Greenbank, and in 1881 it was in the hands of the elderly James Thomas, apparently living alone, a rare situation in nineteenth-century Grundisburgh.

Keeble Pipe, cooper and basketmaker, had lived in Basketmaker's Cottage at Wash (or Pipes') Corner since his father's death in 1850. His business had prospered and in 1881 he was employing 10 men and 3 boys, many of them living round the corner in Half Moon Lane and Vine Cottages.

Near Motum's forge was a house (adjoining Willow Cottage?) originally inhabited by a retired Indian army major, but held in 1861 by a photographer, Will MacLean. With his sister and 4-year-old Charles, he actually lived in a caravan (perhaps beside Weir Pond behind Willow Cottage) while William Barker, aged 25, describing himself as a photographic artist, occupied the house. Weir Pond was filled in after heated debate in 1934 when it had become a popular dumping spot for rubbish.

Grundisburgh Cottage, or The Cottage, opposite Keeble Pipe, had long been the home of Bridget and John Cook who developed the largest firm of general builders in the village, employing six men and a boy in 1861 and later, under his sons and grandsons, up to forty. (He had taken some risks in his time: in 1864 the neighbour of the brick-built Evangelical Chapel at Melton had obtained an order to have the chapel demolished or moved 15 feet since it was obstructing his Ancient Lights. No one else would take on the job of moving it, but Cook did so by means of iron bands and wooden rollers, while his client with commendable faith in Mr Cook and the Almighty, stood throughout in the pulpit.) The Cooks had seven children and all four boys followed in their father's footsteps. John, the youngest, moved into Ivy Cottage, Henry Groom's old home, and in 1888 into Rustic Cottage in Half Moon Lane, which remained in his family until 1959.

Henry Forsdick, brother of George the baker, whose family had rebuilt the post-mill about 1800, was the miller in 1841. In the next 30 years there were five millers. The windmill no doubt lent a character to the village skyline, but, despite being a large mill with three pairs of stones, it (or strictly she) was evidently not very profitable. It had to be boosted when the wind was inadequate by a steam engine, a not uncommon expedient. The miller's house was a modest affair. If the mill's predecessor was the one dismantled by the profit-conscious William Blois, he was probably well-advised.

Hannah and John Lambert ran the Sun inn (now Crest Cottage) in

Weir Pond. (The Jubilee Lamp is on the extreme right of the picture.)

Meeting Lane for around 30 years between 1840 and 1870. They were followed by David Tye and before 1881 by Joseph Dunnett junior, the grocer's son.

At the Half Moon, owned by the Cobbolds, Charles Palmer was landlord during the 1840s and remained there until 1870 when he and his wife moved to become pig dealer and baker respectively on Rose Hill. He was succeeded briefly by Joseph Burch from Clopton who retired to the easier life of a farm labourer, and then by Emma Richardson who carried on until 1904.

During the same 40 years to 1881 the Dog had at least seven landlords. Its owner may have been a poor judge of suitability, perhaps giving undue weight to the age factor since his choices seem to have alternated between young and old. None came from the village nor stayed afterwards. The inn was a relatively large establishment, requiring an ostler, a wife and at least one resident servant, so the overheads may have been too much for the simple needs of the village drinkers. Certainly the Sun was said to be livelier and the beer at the Barley Mow cheaper and better. Even the Vestry at this period seems to have met more often in the Half Moon.

By contrast, the two blacksmiths were the same in 1881 as they had been in 1845, pillars of Hercules on the changing scene round the village green, latterly dominated by the bright red bricks of the new school building beside the church, with its central window latticed for some reason as a star of David.

John and Amy Crapnell at Forge House had eight children, two of whom, William and Mary, were blind. William, who was 30 in

Post-mill.

1881, was still living with his parents and employed, almost certainly by Keeble Pipe, as a basketmaker. Joseph was also at home working at the forge, while John junior, likewise a blacksmith, had settled elsewhere.

The Motums next to the Dog had ten children. Jeremiah, recently widowed, was living with four of them in 1881: Ellen keeping house, William helping at the forge, and Mary and Fred school-teachers. He died at Otley in 1902.

CHAPTER SEVEN

❦
———————————————————

The Poor and the Rich

Among the earliest committee minutes of the Nacton workhouse is a chilling paragraph which mentions the arrival in March 1758 of Samuel Cutting, one of Grundisburgh's overseers, to deliver the poor of the village, 13 in all: 3 in their 70s, 1 of 49, 3 teenagers and 6 children.

The workhouse had just been built to accommodate the deserving poor of the combined Hundreds of Carlford and Colneis, Grundisburgh being in Carlford and Nacton in Colneis. Already there was trouble with the sanitation so that in June the same year an order was given to build a 9 inch wall to separate the latrines (the Bog House, as the clerk put it) from the rest of the building since the stench was causing a great nuisance; and soon there were ominous scrawls in the margins of the weekly register 'smallpox in the house'. A few years later the wooden bedsteads had to be replaced with iron, many of the broken tiles patched up, and the rotten window frames renewed.

Another minute details the unvarying routine of the weekly menus:

	Breakfast	*Dinner*	*Supper*
Sunday	Bread, cheese, butter.	Meat, roots, bread.	Bread and cheese.
Monday	Meat broth.	Baked suet pudding.	Bread and cheese.
Tuesday	Milk broth.	Meat, roots, bread.	Bread and cheese.
Wednesday	Meat broth.	Bread, cheese, butter.	Bread and cheese.
Thursday	Milk broth.	Meat, roots, bread.	Bread and cheese.
Friday	Meat broth.	Bread, cheese, butter.	Bread and cheese.
Saturday	Milk broth, or gruel.	Seed cakes.	Bread and cheese.

"Plus 1 pint of beer, and no more, at each meal." Tea was more popular but it was not available.

After riots outside the workhouse in 1765 – the first of several over the next hundred years – the menus' wording, if not the food, was brightened up as part of a public relations campaign against accusations not only of bad food, foul air in the day rooms and dormitories, and excessive punishments, but also of embezzlement and drunkenness among the staff. Punishment was said to be no more than a restricted diet for swearing, disrepectfulness and similar misdemeanours. There was a set of stocks in the dining room, so that anyone caught lying could be stuck there with a placard round his or her neck saying 'Infamous Lyar'; and although few could read, they surely got the message. There was also a whipping post at Nacton but 'how it came there we know not, and certain it is that it was never used'. As for foul air, the windows were opened daily unless it was raining. And second helpings of food, which was not unreasonably deemed better than anything the paupers might get outside, were always available. But one must not be overpersuaded by bland officialdom. The workhouse was an evil place.

Turnover of inmates, who were categorised as either workers, usually the majority, making sacks and rope, or 'non-effectives' – the old, sick, infants and idiots – was high. Few of Grundisburgh's poor seem to have spent more than a year there before work was found for them outside. Some ran away. One, Elizabeth Capon, aged 51, left to get married. Another, Thomas Loom, was sent to a House of Correction. Many returned. For Adela Garnham who was first delivered at the age of four with her sisters Deborah, Almira and Stella, the workhouse became a home from home.

The same poor families from the village (Loom, Garnham, Mallett, Finch, Worledge) recur with depressing frequency. Some individuals can be identified from the censuses. Mary and Jeremiah Dammant, the ratcatcher, spent a month inside with their 3 children in 1831. John Halls was briefly admitted aged 13 in 1831 and again in 1835 before settling down as a labourer in Lower Road. William Lankester and James Woolnough, both 14, were there for a few months in 1818 when they were apprenticed back in the village as farm labourers; Lankester later became a coal merchant in Half Moon Lane and Woolnough a bricklayer in a cottage near the Dammants behind the present Post Office. Ann Bloomfield, 37, and Sam, aged 13 weeks, arrived for a year's stay in 1834 until they got a cottage near the post-mill; Sam grew up to become a coal carter and father of five, apparently remaining in the same house. Susan and John Graystone, probably the shoemaker beside the Dog between 1841 and 1881, were admitted for a year in 1827.

Seldom indeed does a real person emerge from these bleak records of administered poverty, and it is pure chance which has preserved a letter dated January 1832 from William Worledge, a carpenter living in London, to the Grundisburgh overseers of the poor. Having been born in the village, he was their responsibility. The previous summer he and his wife had been very ill, and she had died. With two children to support, he had received relief from Grundisburgh of 10 shillings a week until he was able to work again. Then:

> 'GENTLEMEN, I hope you will not be offended of me writing to you to let you know my melancholy distress, for I have been out of work ever since a week before Christmas on account of my job being stopped that would have taken me through the winter . . . When the order came for all hands to stop, I thought I should go out of my mind for I knew there were no other jobs in hand. I left my tools there at the shop. I was with the foreman and he told me I should be the first man that was put on, as my tools were there, and he was sure of a larger job as soon as the Christmas business was a little settled.
>
> There must be plenty of work in the City next summer and my master is in middle of it, which may be a lead for me. My mother and sister are wishing I should come home but I am sure there are too many carpenters in Grundisburgh . . . London is such a place if you have not a handful of money. You cannot get anything for rent, and shoes take almost all my money away for myself and 2 children, and are not so good in London as they are in the country unless you go to a great price and I cannot do that. I am almost barefoot at this time and I cannot go a-robbing for anything, and walk about half-starved. I have not written to you till the last moment for I thought something would turn up . . . . I paid 12 shillings for rent, and is now due 8 shillings and must be paid or turned out, and I lose what few things I have. So I changed the last half-crown (30 pence) I had to get this paper. Gentlemen, I would rather go through an operation this New Year's morning than to trouble you for anything but I cannot help it, and I had rather be at work ten times over. Therefore, Gentlemen, if you will be so kind as to take up my awful case in your consideration once more and send me £2, I will be much obliged.'

He seems to have got his money and to reappear lodging in Grundisburgh in the 1841 census.

Apprenticeships, so-called, were compulsory for pauper children over 13, usually as farm labourers and maid-servants. It was up to the overseers of the poor to find them a home in the village, and a premium of five guineas (105 shillings) was offered with each one. The penalty for refusing an offer was £10 which could be added to the premium to sweeten the pill for the next offeree, and so on till the child was placed. There is no record of how high the bidding might go for a really unpromising apprentice. The Rectory must have seemed a good home for difficult cases, but at least one incumbent,

Dr. Ramsden, was too smart for that, and between 1822 and 1824 he paid the penalty four times; or he may have been trying to find the children a better placement.

Even if you made a mistake and took on a dud, it was permitted to pass him or her onto a neighbour together with the premium plus inevitably a further bribe. People who were hard up were thus tempted to take on apprentices who were awkward to place simply to get the money, often the cause of much misery for the children. That may have happened with Lydia Finch, twice apprenticed in 1793 and 1795. She never married and appears to have remained a charge on the parish in her cottage near the chapel until her death in the 1860s.

Children accounted for about 40 per cent of the workhouse inmates, providing a steady flow of apprentices, two or three a year in Grundisburgh's case, whose contribution of paupers at any one time was usually about a dozen. The grim cartload delivered by Samuel Cutting in 1758 was thus typical.

The English welfare state had been the envy of Europe since the Elizabethan Poor Laws had made paupers a charge on their parish of birth, financed by a property tax, or poor rate, for which initially up to twopence in the pound had been enough. The churchwardens helped by a couple of overseers (later four) were responsible for the collection and distribution of money for relief as well as for the provision of a Poor House for the really desperate, which in Grundisburgh was probably one of the cottages behind the Baptist chapel, later known as the Town House (now Rose Cottage?).

The earliest accounts of Grundisburgh's overseers go back to 1660 when poor relief cost £15 for eleven recipients. By 1700 it was £78 and by 1750, after a series of bad harvests, £150. It was this escalation nationwide which encouraged the bright idea that workhouses, of which Nacton was one of the first, would be better value.

Over the years a growing social conscience, strengthened by a healthy fear of riot and contagious disease, had relaxed the dole's original strict conditions. The concept of a subsistence wage gained ground, so that out-relief (as distinct from indoor relief received in goods and services at the workhouse) was increasingly being paid to supplement low farm wages, while the farmers' knowledge that this would happen began a vicious downward spiral. The line, hairs-breadth but administratively vital, between the poor person and the pauper became even fainter when the paupers stopped bothering to sow the P badge onto their clothes as the law demanded, and got away with it.

Subsistence around 1825 was regarded as 14 shillings a week for a family of five children (say £30 today); the father for example earning

9 shillings, the mother 1 shilling, and the children 4 shillings between them. Nine shillings of this was in theory spent on bread, a shilling on potatoes, a shilling on rent and 9 pence on fuel, with the balance going on butter, cheese, tea, soap, etc. Nothing was said about meat, free only for those with poaching skills. Bread, of which the working man was estimated to consume over 3 lbs a day, cost about 3 pence for the equivalent of a 2 lb. loaf, not so much cheaper relative to his wages than for his Domesday forebears. Cheese was about 6 pence a pound and butter double. There was a flourishing market in second-hand tea leaves.

Continued escalating costs produced further action. In 1834 Parliament limited out-relief primarily to the sick and aged, and tightened up the diet and discipline of the workhouse to discourage the supposedly work-shy. The brewing plant at Nacton was ordered to be sold immediately. In Grundisburgh at least, this had some effect and despite the village's doubled population since the mid-1700s, inmates at Nacton (now widened as part of the Woodbridge Union) remained on average around a dozen; while the poor rate which had been £714 in 1832 (about 10 shillings in the pound on an old assessment) halved by 1842.

The actual numbers receiving some form of out-relief in the village varied a good deal, especially after the new Poor Act: in the week to 23 May 1834 nearly £9 was disbursed among 60 names plus the 'widows' list'; in a November week the following year it was under £6 among 27 names plus the widows.

The 1851 census records only 25 paupers, those people more or less wholly dependent on out-relief. The word 'pauper' was in any case beginning to go out of use, soon to be replaced by the new officialese 'unemployed'. Henry Heath who was living two doors away from the Sun in 1871 and seems to have married its recently widowed landlady, herself now out of a job, was the first man to be so described in Grundisburgh. There are no paupers in the 1871 census, people being referred to by their most recent occupation, however part-time.

Charwomen and laundresses begin to pop up everywhere: Emma Spon and Marion Payne in Lower Road in 1861; Jane and Rachel Foulger nearby in 1871; Mary King in Lower Road with Eliza Smith and Eliza Maddison in Half Moon Lane in 1881, not forgetting Mary Foulger from Thistleton and Sarah Pinner at the top of Rose Hill. Cleanliness was becoming a growth industry. The laundry charge was 6 pence for a dozen articles. There was also the Hall's private Laundry House: it is still there, just below the Village Hall with its tied cottage behind it. It was built by Sir Brampton Gurdon to provide a home and employment for Mary Copping after her husband had been killed in a road accident on Tuddenham Hill.

The relieving officer who took over the distribution of out-relief from the parish overseers in 1835 was an altogether tougher proposition. It is clear from his random notes that few poor families escaped without a cut of at least 6 pence in their 2 or 3 shilling dole. Elizabeth Bird's money went down from 7 shillings to 2 shillings plus 28 lbs. of flour worth 3 shillings; she lived in a rent-free cottage with 5 children, two of whom brought home 5 shillings between them. The case of William Cotton, also with five children, was dismissed because the family was earning a total of 10 shillings; no nonsense now about a subsistence wage. Caroline Robinson, an unmarried mother with a new baby and living with a prostitute aunt, was told the baby must go into the workhouse as soon as possible and given 2 shillings a week meantime. Maria Finch, another unmarried mother, only got 15 pence. The illegitimate Joseph Dunnett (aged 11 but one imagines fending for himself) possibly the later woodman and grocer at The Firs, got 2 shillings. Mary Hadley, a nurse earning 5 shillings a week with two children, received 18 pence which was doubled with 14 lbs. of flour when one of them was ill.

The Loom family, relations of Eli, the butcher at the top of Meeting Lane (an area where many of the poorest cottages were gathered which were not attached to farms in the north of the parish) make regular appearances: Charlotte, aged 14, was ordered to the workhouse because her father couldn't support her; Elizabeth, whose husband had been deported for 14 years for stealing chickens and who was now living with the father of her two children, had her allowance discontinued and the children sent to the workhouse; Sarah, 67, was allowed 11 pence a week, and Honor, 68 and sick, 2 shillings.

Medical attention came free to recipients of relief, although it was not always as prompt as the NHS. Mrs. Aaron Lankester, another family much in evidence, complained that the doctor had taken too long to visit her sick, in fact dying, child. That was probably Dr. Acton from Greenbank, retained by the workhouse at £100 a year, about whom several similar complaints are recorded. 'I know where the damned old woman lives,' he exclaimed one Tuesday when called to the bedside of a sick pauper, but he didn't visit her till Friday. He remained, however, on the workhouse payroll.

So much for the deserving poor. For the undeserving poor, such as vagrants and other trouble-makers, there was the House of Correction at Woodbridge (a workhouse without the trimmings) or of course prison. Theft as a rule was confined to farm animals for the simple reason that there was little else to steal. And at least in the nineteenth century, the strong Baptist influence seems to have made serious crime comparatively rare in Grundisburgh.

The parish constable, until the police variety was embodied in the 1840s, had for many centuries been responsible for law and order, as well as supervision of the militia and the collection of taxes. Like other officials he was elected annually by the Vestry and confirmed by the rubber stamp of a magistrate. It could be a dangerous and tedious job, but one of great dramatic interest, and most unfortunately none of the Grundisburgh records has survived.

The poor of Grundisburgh never had much joy out of established charities. The income of the Town Lands, or Town Estate (chiefly from fields north of Bast's plus a few cottages) which was the successor of the medieval guild, grew from £3 or so to £60 between 1600 and 1900; and at least in the later years, three-quarters of that went to the church and only a quarter to the most needy households in the parish, who received, in addition to soup on certain occasions, up to 5 cwt. of coal each winter. (Now they get electricity vouchers.) The gift of a pair of boots to James Saunders to help him get out of the parish for at least 10 years was an exceptional item.

Robert Thinge, whose legacy in 1731 rebuilt the church tower, left the poor a shilling's worth of bread a week 'for ever'; John Lucock of Grundisburgh House in 1821 left £15 a year, £10 for bread and coal and £5 (a generous wage) to pay a Sunday school teacher; and Samuel Dawson of Burgh in 1863 £6 annually for coal, the three of them now all but swept away by the lethal combination of bureaucracy and inflation. Lucock, for example, left capital of £300 invested in 5 per cent Annuities: by 1896 the income had fallen to under £8 of which the Charity Commission ruled £5 must still go to the church. Only the Gurdon Trust, endowed by Sir Brampton in 1897 with seven cottages (Vine Cottages near the present Rectory and 1–3 Chapel Row) now administers an income (currently over £10,000) comparable in real terms to what may have been the most generous, if unwitting, benefaction of all, from Roger Palmer.

Roger in his will of 1445 seems to have left Bast's to his step-daughter Agnes Gosslyn, on condition she donated £20 a year to the church for seven years. She evidently decided it wasn't worth it and the estate passed to the guild trustees. Thomas Wall, the City salter, who we know rebuilt the house in about 1520 (and rather vulgarly had a salt cellar carved on one of its posts) had only some sort of lease on it with a strangely unenforceable option for his daughter Katherine to purchase after his death; and it was possibly some muddle over this which caused her to buy and sell Grundisburgh Hall in the 1550s. In any case, Bast's was sold eventually and the proceeds hopefully devoted, as Roger had stipulated, to charity.

Agnes Gosslyn's rejection somehow sets the scene on the long decline of Bast's, Grundisburgh's most famous house. The present building, perhaps too grand for the small farm once attached to it, has spent most of its life in the occupation of tenants or sub-tenants of absentee landlords, at length being left virtually derelict during the First World War after it had been sold by the Busks who had owned it since at least the eighteenth century. The Tudor and Jacobean panelling is now elsewhere, the old porch has gone, the roof was remodelled over a hundred years ago, and the windows and chimney stacks, however authentic from a distance, are vintage twentieth century; while the Bast family, so fertile in the middle ages, on whose land Roger Palmer's house was built, is long extinct.

Only in recent years has the house revived, minus most of its land, under the love and care it no doubt once received from Thomas Wall and his distinguished heirs, the Colets. Katherine married John, cousin of Dean Colet, founder of London's St. Paul's school, the man who first justified the Reformation to Erasmus (an important break-through for the authorities) and the family remained in Grundisburgh, perhaps in Bast's, for at least two generations thereafter. Katherine's grand-daughter married George Joury with a little property at the bottom of Stoney Road.

Charities were few in Grundisburgh because rich men were few, almost non-existent as the world goes, apart from the lords of the manor. Thomas Wall, whose ancestry in the village went back a hundred years, had a lot of money and, like his near-contemporary Richard Blois, he had probably made most of it himself. Grundisburgh was where they lived, but their wealth came from elsewhere and mostly remained there.

The Thinge family were prosperous grocers but it is hard to believe they could have made a real fortune locally from that; and Robert's will indicates they were far from being in the same league as the Walls. Robert occupied none of the properties mentioned in his will, and, as we know that at some period the Thinges lived in Bast's, it is possible that he, as well as his grandfather, was a tenant of the house.

Likewise the farming families: with several servants, pleasant houses and plenty to eat, they were rich only in strictly relative terms. Some of them, notably the Harrises, the Manbys and the Bedwells, had been at it for the best part of a century or more when the young Queen was crowned in 1838 (an event celebrated in the Nacton workhouse with plum pudding) and this continuity persisted through the six following censuses. Although they were only tenant farmers, all of them had had time to build up some capital, of which around £10 per acre would have been required as working capital on the farm.

During the 1840s a new generation took over the village's three largest farms, all Gurdon-owned: Philip Harris at Park Farm (270 acres), the only one near the average size for Suffolk, having its own forge and employing just nine men, with George Ablitt at Wood Farm and James Burch at Elm Tree, both less economic units on about 200 acres and employing eight men. All three farmers had succeeded their fathers, although James Burch in his 50s was a generation older than the other two.

Henry Manby was tenant of the 113 acres of Hill Farm where he had followed his grandfather, while his mother and brother John farmed about the same acreage at Bast's, which included 21 acres leased from the Town Estate. Henry's wife died in 1844, as did John just afterwards, so Henry moved to Bast's. Later, on his retirement to Hillingdon on Rose Hill, he installed John Watson, one of his farm employees, at Bast's as manager. Watson was soon back in his

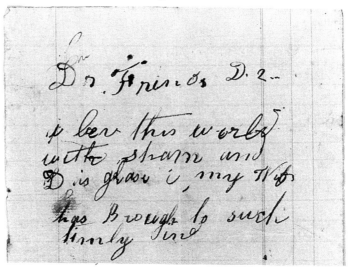

James Upson's suicide note.

cottage, replaced by Henry Hawes until another Manby, Tom, took it over in the early 1880s, shortly to begin an eventually successful battle to screw a lower rent out of the Town Estate.

At Brook Farm, 24 acres owned by a family of Woodbridge solicitors, John Bedwell died in 1838 and was succeeded by his 19-year-old son Ben. This farm, once owned by Robert Thinge, was charged with providing the poor with their shilling's worth of bread each Sunday. Ben, who was clearly a man of energy – parish clerk and four times census enumerator – soon expanded to 65 acres, probably taking over neighbouring Barn Farm after James Upson's suicide in 1845. He purchased Brook Farm itself in 1866. Finally, on James Burch's death in 1873 he moved for a time to Elm Tree Farm, which gave him a good unit of 260 acres altogether.

James Upson, the brother of Maria Parker of the Bricklayer's Arms, had hanged himself in his bedroom one evening after work, having stuffed a note in his breeches' pocket mentioning his shame and disgrace. He was known to have serious money problems, but the Rector, Mr. Webster, wrote privately to the coroner blaming an unnamed woman ('you know who I mean').

Near Bond's Corner, the lonely uplands cross-roads towards Otley where one can well believe the legend of the eponymous suicide's grave, John Harris (Philip's uncle) was the tenant of Poplar Farm in 1841. His neighbours were Joseph Groom, the former butcher on Rose Hill who moved to Whitehouse Farm in the 1840s, and Mrs. Groom's relations, the Newsons, at Bond's Corner itself. They both left in about 1865 and it looks as if Harris then took on all three farms, 421 acres together; but he died a few years later – it was a bad time to expand – and his family reverted to Poplar alone which at some stage they had purchased. The farm was subsequently acquired by Philip from his uncle's estate for £4000. When it was sold some 40 years later in the depths of the depression, it fetched £900.

Thomas Read, and later his son William who died in 1916, were the only self-styled gentlemen-farmers in the village, owning the 105 acres of Bridge Farm on the Woodbridge Road. His wife inherited the property from a great-aunt who had bought it from an unsuccessful gambler called Mr. Dove.

Grundisburgh House is believed to have been built around 1700 by the Bloises as a residence for their agent. It was bought in 1793 by Thomas Smith, a schoolmaster, and in 1802 by a London pawnbroker and allegedly slum property dealer, the charitable John Lucock, who added the grand Regency façade. And, on the other side of Wash Corner, his brother, gentleman on his tombstone but before that a successful City hairdresser, clumsily enlarged Finndale House in a similar style but on a more modest scale.

During the forty years that the Gurdons were living at Letton in the mid-nineteenth century, Grundisburgh Hall was leased to various tenants, only two of whom appear in the censuses: the Colchesters, Harwich shipowners, and the Frasers, Ipswich rag-trade.

When Brampton Dillingham bought the Grundisburgh Hall estate in 1772, he charged his farm tenants an average of under 15 shillings an acre, which by 1820 had risen to nearer 25 shillings, the figure that Henry Manby and his grandfather had been paying for thirty years at Hill Farm. It is debatable whether, over a period, the farmers made

'A spot so very beautiful.' Grundisburgh Hall from the south-west.

as much money out of their land as did their landlords with less risk. A tenant of 100 acres was probably no better off than Mr Dobrée, the curate, with his stipend of £120 a year or Henry Wright, the workhouse relieving officer, neither of them outstanding examples of affluence.

There were certainly occasions when the Gurdons agreed to forgo part of their rent, sometimes adding a reminder of the 'enormous profits' the farmer should have made during the Napoleonic Wars. An extra shilling a week for the men could well have cut 10 per cent off a farm's profit, one of several reasons why the farmers, in spite of government propaganda, were keen to keep wages low. Would lower rents have helped? No one then seriously thought to challenge the hidden hand of capitalist economics, or was equipped to do so. Mr. Dillingham expected a return of 3½ per cent on his money in the 1770s and Henry Manby's landlady at Hill Farm 4 per cent in the 1840s, the market rate; and that was that.

CHAPTER EIGHT

The Schools

Mr. Redit spent the day in school as usual. Then, having consumed 'a quantity' of his wife's home-made wine, followed by 25 drops of laudanum, he went up to his attic bedroom where, during the night, he cut his throat with a penknife. He had not been himself recently, and only that day had told his daughter 'If I go on in this way I shall soon be in the asylum.' On the strength of that, the coroner qualified his verdict of suicide with 'lunatic', thereby enabling the body to be buried in St. Mary's churchyard. Such, in February 1832, was the sad end of Grundisburgh's first professional schoolmaster of whom we have any information.

As a young man he had started as an assistant at Mrs. Smith's girls' school, already well established in Grundisburgh at the end of the eighteenth century. (She may have been the Mrs. Smith of Grundisburgh House.) He had become headmaster in 1805, switching to boys only and changing its name from Smith's to Grundisburgh School. It was situated at Bridge House on the south side of the green, the schoolroom in a separate building at the back. After his death it was taken over by Edward and Phoebe Robinson, and continued to flourish until Edward's death in 1858. The boarding fees were 18 guineas (nearly £19) per annum.

The news of Nathaniel Redit's suicide reached the ears of the redoubtable Mrs. Frere in Cambridge, Brampton Dillingham's daughter and now the wife of the Master of Downing. Her father, ahead of his time in educational perception as in architectural taste, had presented the parish with a schoolroom, on the site of the present Parish Rooms but shorter and narrower, which had been run by Sarah and Herman Groom (he of the 18 children, several by another wife after Sarah) until some time in the 1820s. Mr. Dillingham was dead by then, and Herman, who lived at Ivy Cottage next door to the schoolroom, fell back on his earlier trade, turning the school into his carpenter's shop. This Mrs. Frere now arranged to revert to its original purpose. Her initiative was rather feebly welcomed by Mr.

Grundisburgh Hall: Mr. Dillingham's Regency front.

Webster, the new Rector, who admitted there were 15 children in the village who should benefit from a bit of education.

The schoolroom remained operational for the next forty years, during much of that time under the control (the not very efficient control, according to a note by Sir Brampton Gurdon among the family papers) of another Sarah Groom, wife of William the former blacksmith who was living opposite Forge House in 1851.

The education was free, financed by the Rector, and after about 1860 by the National Society for Promoting the Education of the Poor in the Principles of the Established Church, a government-supported organisation in urgent need of an acronym. Mrs. Groom's salary was £12 a year. She also took Sunday school, mostly the children she had taught during the week, for which she would have received John Lucock's annual fiver.

Official figures claim that in 1833, 158 children attended school in Grundisburgh. They were by no means all from the village: 91 were at the three private schools where all the boarders and some of the day pupils would have come from elsewhere. In any case, the actual numbers in school on any one day would surely have been below 100. The children's priority was to earn, not learn. The refurbished free parochial school, whose planned capacity was 40, is said to have had 67 pupils in 1833. Again, a large proportion must have come from outside the village unless Mr Webster's original estimate was hopelessly inaccurate; 22 out of 38 had done so in 1818. In the same year (1833) the Baptists had 75 at their Sunday school, half the figure of 15 years earlier in the days of Pastor Thompson. Grundisburgh's population in the 5–12 age group was around 160 in 1833.

Private schools were usually the so-called dame schools, charging about 3 pence a week for day pupils and specialising in younger children. In what may not be typical examples, Mrs. Forsdick and Miss Steggall, the Rose Hill rivals of the 1870s, on one occasion had 22 pupils between them, 5 boys and 17 girls. The 1841–81 censuses show that during that period there was always at least one dame school in the village (there were six in 1818) apart from the Robinsons': as a husband and wife team with one or more assistants, and taking boys up to 14, theirs was not a dame school at all, and very much a cut above them as the fees indicate. They almost all took boarders who, as is still the case, provided the financial icing on the cake. On the chance date of the censuses, obviously a crude guide, Mrs. Knights at Brooklands had the highest score during those forty years with six. The Robinsons had three boarders in the 1841 census and a solitary 10-year-old in 1851 who, if he was really the only one, must have found life very dull in the evenings.

What they were taught at these schools was pretty basic. The father of Elizabeth Garrett Anderson, Newson Garrett, whose own parents lived at Leiston, was educated in Grundisburgh, almost certainly at Redit's, and grew up with a minimal writing ability. One of the crazier suggestions put forward in connection with workhouse schools in 1836 was that pauper children should be taught to read but not write, to prevent them having an unfair advantage over those outside. Nevertheless, it has been estimated that half the adult population of Suffolk could at least write their own names by 1850 and three-quarters by 1875.

To respond to this rising tide of literacy, the Education Act of 1870 set up a programme of school building, each to be managed by its own Board; non-denominational, which caused a great rumpus throughout the Church. The Board for Grundisburgh and Burgh was formed in 1873.

Mr. Turner, Rector of Grundisburgh, and Mr Fraser, tenant of the Hall, both excused themselves through indisposition from the stone-laying ceremony on land acquired next to the church from the owner of Bast's; and only the threat by one of the Harrises that he would break into the church tower and ring the bells himself produced the compromise of a brief and feeble peal through the pouring rain. In spite of everything there was a good turnout of parents and children. They sang 'All people that on earth do dwell'

Robert Gurdon, first Lord Cranworth.

and Robert Gurdon, representing his father, absentee landlord but still lord of the manor, having laid the foundation stone, made a neat little speech. 'However lowly your lot,' he told them, 'there are others whose lot is lowlier still.' After three cheers for Mr. Gurdon, the School Board and themselves, they sang another hymn and went home to change their clothes.

The school, with the headmaster's half-completed house adjoining, opened in 1875, 'an ornament to the parish', its design, especially the flèche or mini-spire housing the school bell (to some modern eyes the worst feature of an undistinguished building) being favourably compared to the 'rather ugly' church tower beside it.

There were 160 pupils on the books, over 80 per cent of the entire school-age population of the two villages (but children may also have come from Culpho and Hasketon) and attendance in Week One averaged 123. Numbers increased over the years, partly as a result of compulsory attendance after 1880, reinforced by a £2 penalty for employing schoolchildren, and partly because in the early years pupils were often allowed to leave school at 11 plus – 13 being the official age – once they had reached a certain, not necessarily the same, standard.

Parents paid school fees according to their means: some none at all, most a penny a week, until payment was abolished in 1891. It was too much hassle to collect, and there was little you could do about arrears except refuse to let the child leave early, which made matters worse. The actual cost of running the school was reckoned to be cheap at 7 pence per child per week.

'The children knew practically nothing,' wrote Mr. Blackmore, the headmaster, 'many from 9–12 not even knowing the alphabet, and of course having no idea of arithmetic.' He soon had them 'drilling in numeration' and learning instructive songs, 'The Vowels', 'Speak the Truth', 'Our Flag to Save' and others. Singing and needlework became features of the school. The girls did needlework under Mrs. Blackmore instead of geography and were regular prizewinners in the district. Five 'inefficient' monitors, 11- and 12-year-olds at the top of the school, who did at least know their alphabet, helped her teach the infant classes, receiving a shilling a week for their trouble.

Emma and Walter Blackmore, who were certified teachers in their mid-twenties in 1875, had no other help apart from a couple of 13-year-old pupil-teachers (that is, trainee teachers, as distinct from monitors), Frances Buttrum and Fred Motum, the blacksmith's son, who also had to be taught after school. Fred was weak on Euclid and Frances on spelling.

It would be interesting to know where the older children had received their previous education. The Robinsons' establishment had closed 17 years ago. Sarah Groom, older than the century, had retired from the parochial school in about 1870, giving place to young Mary Ann Ward, so standards there may have improved. Or was there some better school in a neighbouring parish?

Poor attendance, the result of parental indifference, was one of Mr. Blackmore's headaches. Numbers dropped drastically on rainy days, or if there was a pigeon match, or when the children were required in the fields for stone-picking, or for multifarious other reasons. In 1883 he introduced Reward Cards which for a time reduced absenteeism from 85 to an average of 40 a day: one card for every four weeks' full attendance, eight cards a year winning a prize. The system lasted for many years. It was difficult, without seeming to take off the pressure, to drop it.

By 1897, when the Blackmores were forced to resign because of Emma's ill-health, the Inspectorate had rated the school one of the best in Suffolk on the basis of their three criteria of academic standard, attendance and care of the building's fabric. As cheap materials had been used, this last was quite important.

The Blackmores' pay was a basic £101 a year plus bonus depending on the Inspectors' report, which for some years had produced an aggregate salary of £163, the maximum allowed under the Act. There were five pupil-teachers by now, on around £30 a year, and

Mrs. Hardy.

just two monitors on £5 each. The unsatisfactory monitor system
was ended a few months later.

The remuneration of their successors, Mr. and Mrs. Josiah Hardy,
was £160 a year with no bonus, a deal which certainly turned out
favourably for them. Jo Hardy was not popular with the children,
and at least in the later years their results were poor; and after his
death in 1926 the Board were moved to record a 'vast improvement
in the school' during the two years following.

Mr Hardy at once set about making it clear he didn't share the
Inspectors' high regard for the competence of his new pupils. He
noted that writing in the school was very fair; tables poor; spelling
fair; book-work very poor, especially sums; model-drawing very
poor. Reading and mental arithmetic were good. Only singing was
very good. History and geography apparently were not worth
mentioning. 'Needlework', said Mrs. Hardy, was 'too fine'. So
much for the Blackmores and their bonuses.

Mrs. Hardy, who asked that her 40 per cent share of their salary be
paid into a separate account, clearly had a way with her and the
knack of projecting it, and her manifold problems, onto paper. She
was a reluctant teacher and, with three children of her own, spent
much of her time on administration. 'Children have stopped away',
she wrote, 'as if there were no Attendance Officer.' The wretched
man 'seems to think attendance is alright . . . For the first time he

Mr Hardy speaking at the flower show about 1923. Lady Cranworth presenting the prizes.

brought last week's form with him.' (His main job, of course, was visiting delinquent households, not being agreeable to Mrs. Hardy.) H. Kirk, an assistant teacher, 'has done just what suited him . . . his scripture lessons are only time wasted, and in 8 weeks he has taught nothing'. He and another teacher who 'has made backwards progress' were given a month's notice. 'At my wits' end', she records, 'at the bad methods and slipshod ways of two trained arithmetic teachers.'

The cleaner was unpunctual and 'crams the stove full of coke though I have warned him'. The dentist, on the other hand, was too punctual: 'impossible to have the cards ready'. Even Mrs. Round-Turner, former chatelaine of Grundisburgh House and relict of the naval captain to whose memory St. Mary's pulpit is dedicated, comes in for stick: the old lady had hired the school hall for a concert, and the next morning a window was smashed and the new desks scratched, having obviously been 'stood upon'.

The children themselves seemed less trouble: the Andrews with their nits, the dirty couple who had come to her from Woodbridge School, the two she 'put out' of her gardening class for destroying cauliflowers, the boy who said his parents didn't want him to do PE: 'I gave him a good punishment and promised to repeat it.' Little escaped her eagle eye or avenging pen.

In 1908 the relative calm of the village was confounded by the arrival at their new Home of a dozen workhouse children. Twenty-five years earlier it had been arranged that pauper children who couldn't be boarded out with foster-families should be housed together at St. John's Home in Ipswich. It was felt they were being institutionalised by the desperate atmosphere of the Nacton and other workhouses, although St. John's, with 235 beds, seems in some ways hardly better. (One boy – not at Nacton – when asked about his ambition in life is said to have replied that it was to join the men's side of the workhouse where he would have more freedom.) Now, however, St. John's was to be entirely limited to Ipswich children, and perhaps on the initiative of Walter Blackmore who was on the committee, Street Farmhouse on Grundisburgh green at the bottom of Meeting Lane was taken over.

The Matron took one look at her new charges and resigned. It has been suggested that the real reason may have been the 'help' provided by the sub-committee of the Home, nearly as numerous as the children it was planned to contain. Or it may have been the prospect of too little help, in fact virtually none, other than from the children themselves. Her replacement, who arrived after a tricky interlude, seems to have been a minimalist in terms of both food and supervision, which she largely left to the older children. Certainly the Home acquired the dubious reputation of being the most economical in the district.

To be fair to both matron and children, the regime and ethos of the Home derived from those of the workhouse of which it was still a part.

Every day in term time a well-dressed crocodile crossed the green to school, no problem for the Attendance Officer at any rate. There is a story of one little girl in about 1924 who was so thin and frail that Mr. Hardy excused her from PE. She evidently received no comparable consideration at the Home, where she could be seen hard at housework with the best of them, staggering under a washing basket to and from the clothes line. One morning she failed to appear at breakfast and Matron stormed upstairs to deal with the malingerer only to find she had died in the night.

Whatever the friction inside the Home, outside the children stuck fiercely together, and woe betide the village boy or girl who fell foul of any one of them. They met their match, however, in the Rector, Mr. Sutton, who, having once caught them stealing his apples, made them eat the lot then and there. Another time, a boy climbed onto the roof of the church tower, and after a brief shouting match (Mr. Sutton's voice croaked rather than carried) Jo Hardy's advice was sought. 'He'll come down when he's hungry,' he said.

The shop at Thatched Cottage.

In 1923 the children, now 24 in number, were given 3 pence a week pocket money, a revolutionary boost for them and the village sweet shops, one, Alexanders, near the Dog, the other, Dimmocks, at Thatched Cottage opposite the Half Moon. It was further away but had the dual attractions of relationship to a famous football player and the reputed residence of a ghost.

The Home was closed in 1938 and the children dispersed to other establishments, no doubt larger and still more economical. During the war it was turned into a nursing home and thereafter into a private house, now ingeniously named The Holme.

The Board school had three headmasters in the thirteen years between the death of Jo Hardy and the outbreak of the Second World War. Holidays had got longer (they were nine weeks a year before the first war), a wireless was introduced in 1933 (a generous gift costing £10) and evening classes, originally intended under the 1870 Act as a form of additional education in the three R's for teenagers, were developed on modern lines: gentle subjects at first, home nursing, cookery, woodwork and veterinary science; later, boxing, folk-dancing and drama were added. Fifty-three enrolled for the opening classes. New crimes, gum-chewing and smoking, began to appear in the Punishment Book, for which two or three strokes on the hand was the standard retribution.

With the war came the evacuees. No question this time, as there had been in 1916, of digging up half the playground for potatoes. Ten teachers and 167 children were added to the 126 locals (families were smaller now) with their five teachers. They kept themselves separate, using the school in shifts, taking turns for mornings or afternoons on alternate weeks. Fortunately many evacuees returned home at the start of the Blitz, and soon the Women's Institute and the Baptists' Sunday schoolroom were made available for the remainder. Eighteen survived to celebrate VE Day in Grundisburgh, but by then they had all been absorbed into the village school.

View from the Half Moon towards Wash Corner, about 1920.

By 1947, when the leaving age was raised to 15, Grundisburgh was categorised as a primary school to age 11, after which pupils were to go on (once the building was ready, which took some years) to free secondary education in Woodbridge, the great educational break-through of our time.

In the same year it was announced that Grundisburgh school was to be rebuilt on a more spacious site; and so it was, 42 years later.

Miss Ward's parochial school closed when the Board school opened. The building became the Village Club and Reading Room, open to men only, age 15 and over, from 7 to 9 o'clock every weekday evening between October and April for an annual subscription of 3 shillings.

Apart from a portrait of the Queen and a map of Palestine (left over from Mrs Groom's Sunday school?) it contained a dozen chairs round a single table plus shelves which ultimately held 150 books changed yearly by its parent body, the Suffolk Association of Village Clubs. They could be borrowed for 6 pence a quarter. Mr. Webster had provided the same service for nothing from his own, perhaps more specialist, library. The *East Anglian Daily Times* was taken in, and a variety of magazines donated, doubtless back numbers, enhancing the general atmosphere of a dentist's waiting room.

Draughts, chess, solitaire and bagatelle were also available. Draughts was Grundisburgh's game and every year a prize tournament was held. At no time was smoking, gambling or bad language permitted. Cocoa and coffee drinking were allowed after 1887 and playing cards after 1897.

Unsurprisingly, this refined austerity rather put off the very people it was aimed at, 'the labouring population', and from the beginning it was dominated by tradespeople and retired folk; a former War Office clerk, Frederick Crafer of Finndale House – then called The Villa – was its first President. The Club seems to have been his brainchild. As a result membership was never adequate. Captain Round-Turner organised fund-raising events to relieve a chronic insolvency, and the room was hired out to organisations like Fred Motum's sickness insurance society, the Gurdon Lodge of Oddfellows, who after a time returned to their more convenient, and more convivial, venue at the Dog. The line was drawn at lending the room to the Relieving Officer for distribution of the weekly dole, a nice indication of gentility and perhaps of his lack of official funds to pay the rent. It would have been a more comfortable alternative to the church porch, the traditional administrative centre of the village.

In 1885 a serious attempt was made to broaden the Club's appeal. A room was added at the east end as a separate Reading Room, the age of entry was lowered to 13 and a quoits group formed. It was felt that quoits would keep the Club together during the summer months, another example of the clique mentality; but it boosted membership from around 40 to a record 58.

Six years later, Robert Gurdon – 'rather unwisely', according to Sir Brampton, his younger brother – allowed the Rector to enlarge the building. The front wall was moved 4 feet nearer the road and another storey added as a Parish Room entirely for the church's use, which seems in the event to have been chiefly limited to Sunday school, school dinners, and the Mothers' Union. At the same time the name was changed to Village Club and Institute. Books were still obtainable, although thanks to a gift from Mrs. Round-Turner, the billiard table was now the main attraction. At the beginning of the First World War the building was taken over by the army and left a total shambles after it.

It was reopened in 1919 with a new billiard table and other equipment provided as compensation by the War Department. 'The labouring population' now had half a day off a week and the emphasis was on football, cricket, darts and table tennis. There was a football field on one of the Town Estate fields behind Bast's. Among the less energetic, draughts was still popular, together with whist drives for which in 1934 ladies were admitted by invitation. Even so, numbers fell. Many failed to pay their subscriptions (now only 30 pence) and insolvency again loomed.

The Club closed for good in 1941 when the building became the Home Guard HQ. It has remained without a real purpose ever since, only a reminder of Brampton Dillingham's foresight 200 years ago. And the Jubilee Lamp, errected by members' subscription in 1887 in the street outside, has gone likewise.

CHAPTER NINE

———————— ❧ ————————

The Roads

MEDIEVAL roads were mostly bridle tracks. Animals went to market on the hoof and goods were transported by pack-horse. Although carts and wagons were rare on the roads before 1600, the increase in commerce and traffic under the Tudors persuaded Parliament that something must be done about repairs and maintenance. The result was the 1555 Highways Act, almost as unfair in its financial provisions as the poll-tax enactments of Richard II or Mrs Thatcher. They remained, however, essentially unchanged for 280 years.

Anyone with a holding worth £50 or more a year (roughly ten times the agricultural wage) was bound to make a horse and cart available, plus two men, for six consecutive days each year to maintain the highway, while every other able-bodied householder, regardless of means, must provide his own labour for the same period. The penalty for not doing so was 18 pence per day for labour and 10 shillings for horse and cart. By the eighteenth century, inflation had made it more economic for the better-off to pay the fine, provided they had the cash, which in time became formalised as a property tax, the Highways rate, of around 6 pence in the £.

The extant records concerning Grundisburgh's parish highways start in 1757 when there were four Surveyors (two or three after 1766) appointed by the Vestry each year to enforce the Act. Apart from the expense and inconvenience of it all, most farmers, anyway in the earlier years, didn't want better roads, softer going being more suited to their animals; while in the village centre, stepping stones along and across the highway were perfectly adequate for pedestrians. Thus the Act was widely modified or ignored, the main reason why it was tolerated so long.

Moreover it was hard for the Surveyors to exercise much effective control over the work itself. If they were too tough on a farming neighbour, he could get his own back when it was his turn to be a Surveyor, and as for the labourers, lacking any kind of financial or other incentive, many an hour was said to have been spent propping up spades between alcoholic refreshment. Anyhow all they did was fill in pot-holes with sand and gravel, sometimes stones, or more earth; or in extreme cases, plough up a section of road and rake it over.

In practice, roads round the centre of the village were no doubt repaired with little fuss as and when they got too bad. It was different with the present B1079, a busy highway linking Woodbridge and Eye, but one relatively little used by people in Grundisburgh. Nevertheless, between Sarsant's Bridge near Bridge Farm and Burgh Bridge behind Finndale House, it was within the parish, and so under its Surveyors.

The two bridges themselves were another matter. By luck the Grundisburgh Surveyors had accounts to show they had rebuilt Sarsant's Bridge in the summer of 1800, so that it was indisputably in place when Parliament made all existing bridges the county's responsibility in 1803. The question of Burgh Bridge was more uncertain: in 1445 Roger Palmer of Bast's had left 10 shillings for its maintenance, but even if this was its site, there was no evidence of how long it might have survived across a river so easily fordable. Neither it nor Sarsant's Bridge are mentioned in a 1651 list of county bridges, although it is clear from the deeds of Bridge Farm that the latter certainly existed in 1687.

In the mid-1870s, Burgh Bridge, brick built, was swept away in a flood, and the county claimed Grundisburgh and Burgh were responsible for its rebuilding. The ratepayers of the two parishes, faced with a bill of £200, took the case to court and won; but they never actually proved the bridge had been there before 1803.

The Dog, about 1920.

By 1800 the B1079 had become, after heavy investment, a profitable turnpike road, able to pay for its own maintenance, although it was still in theory entitled to a portion of Grundisburgh's labour. Even so, the section through the parish was criticised in 1820 as winding, cut-up and incommodious; and the strange suggestion made that the sharp left-hand bend after Burgh Bridge should be cut off by a new stretch to be constructed behind Grundisburgh Cottage and House, following the river and across its flood-plain, rejoining the existing road beyond Burgh Rectory. (That meadow at Burgh Corner seems to have a special attraction for road planners: a slightly similar suggestion has been made in more recent years.)

The turnpike road was 12 feet wide, and Sarsant's Bridge under 11 feet, about half its present measurement. The Street in Grundisburgh was no wider. The road through the centre of the green wasn't constructed until the early twentieth century, originally with a ford until its bridge was built in 1935.

Town Lane, between Bast's and Grundisburgh House, which in its present condition would have compared favourably with most roads in the parish until this century, never seems to have been more than a short-cut to Burgh across various Town Estate fields. It, too, leads to a bridge over the river, and that could have been the one to which Roger Palmer was referring.

Stoney Road is said to have been made from the rubble of the old tower of the church when it collapsed in the seventeenth century; and Stanaway Farm is named from the 'stone way', the Roman road across its land by Otley College. The names of other roads are of more recent origin. Meeting Lane (originally Meeting House Lane) obviously post-dates the chapel, and Rose Hill has a whiff of genteel Victorian nomenclature.

The 1589 Survey of Grundisburgh manor mentions, without identifying, Wygerhall (Wergenhall?) Way, Cattlys Lane and Sybons Way as well as the High Road. An even older document dated 1536 records a legacy of 80 pence to repair the road between Grundis-burgh Street and Bobet's Forge. During the eighteenth century Flet Cheese Corner (a hard and noxious local product) was the name of the junction of Stoney Road and the track called Green Road leading up to Hill Farm: it curved westward to the north of the farmhouse to rejoin Stoney Road south of Bond's Corner, completing the circle around the old common lands. And Squeech Lane still leads from Pound Corner to the squeech or covert near Elm Tree Farm.

Even today, people are a bit vague about the names of Grundis-burgh's two rivers, and it must be doubted if in previous centuries they took any interest at all in such precision. William Blois (no. 3) referred to the river which flows through Grundisburgh green as the

Rose Hill, mid 1950s, before the road was widened.

brook. Maps now call it the Gull, after Gull Farm, or The Gull, situated beside the brook in a hollow or gully, whose name goes back at least to 1800. The Gull joins the main river, the Lark, behind Grundisburgh House. One or other of them is mentioned in the 1589 Survey simply as the common river. Before the Second World War, the Lark had been called the Fynn, the name by which both streams of that river were known: the Bealings branch (still the Fynn and so described in Domesday) rising near Tuddenham, and the other from Otley flowing through Burgh and Grundisburgh, until the two come together a mile or so from Martlesham Creek.

Public transport in the village was centred on the Dog. An innkeeper is recorded in Grundisburgh in 1697 and there is no reason to suppose he was not the Dog's landlord. Its forecourt was the terminus of the Woodbridge and Ipswich coaches (or wagons), whose horses could be looked after in the stables at the back.

The earliest mention of the Dog itself appears to be during the Napoleonic Wars when it and the Half Moon were designated by the army as billets for twelve men each. The inn's name may conceivably derive from the old story of a ghost-dog, an amorphous white animal, sometimes the size of a bullock, which is said to be seen in these parts before some great personal tragedy. (The last man believed to have seen it was a U.S. airman during the Second World War on the night before he went missing.) It is liable to give chase, especially after closing time.

In 1820 George Forsdick was running a coach between Grundisburgh and Woodbridge every Tuesday and Saturday, and probably to Ipswich on several other days. By 1855 he had two competitors, James Adams of Fenn Cottage in Lower Road and the singing teacher, Will Benningfield. Coaches then ran five days a week to both Woodbridge and Ipswich and back, but not on Thursdays to Ipswich nor Tuesdays to Woodbridge.

Adams continued as the village's main operator until he retired around 1880. His nephew, Thomas, who followed him, set up for a time what looks like a little cartel with the only other carrier, Charles Dunnett, his uncle's neighbour. Adams served the Woodbridge route and Dunnett Ipswich. This enabled them to cut the timetable, and work a four-day week instead of five.

The journey to Ipswich took about 3 hours. The more energetic could walk it in that time. The coach (an enclosed cart which took goods, including livestock, as well as passengers) left the Dog at 9 o'clock in the morning and got back at 7.

Meantime Charles Cotton was switching his interest from steam threshing machines to the internal combustion engine. In the first decade of the twentieth century he opened a garage on Rose Hill in the Parkers' old maltings behind Daisy and Red Cottages. He himself lived three doors up the hill at Red House, in front of which he erected a petrol pump. He owned the first car in the village, a 1902 Benz. He and his son Arthur, who occupied Red Cottage, started the village's first motor bus in 1919, three days to Woodbridge and back, and two to Ipswich. (Daily commuting was thus impossible to either town.) The return fare was 7 pence to Woodbridge and a shilling to Ipswich, comparable to actual modern prices but considerably more expensive relative to wages.

Charles Foulger at the bakery had advertised as a cab proprietor since 1908, and he and the Dunnetts survived as scheduled carriers with horse-drawn vehicles well into the 1920s. By then of course another competitor was firmly established, the bicycle.

CHAPTER TEN

The Twentieth Century

TH E mood of a new century is often set during the 90s of the old one, and in Grundisburgh the 1891 census provides a link between the dry facts of history and the living memories of people still flourishing in the village; (but just as records can vanish, reminiscences can be unprintable). It provides, too, the first mention of the lost generation of the twentieth century, killed in the First World War, thirty-one names on the War Memorial, 1 in 10 of every man and boy in the village and over a quarter of those of military age.

Eagerly they had volunteered in 1914 and, mustered on the green, were inspected by Lord Cranworth. Among them was Peter Harris, already a trained soldier and an accomplished poacher. 'So you're off

Dedication of the War Memorial by Mr. Sutton. His son's is one of the names on it. Lord Cranworth, whose son's name was added after World War II, standing behind the Rector.

to kill some Germans, Harris,' said Lord Cranworth. 'If I can hit your pheasants,' he replied, 'I reckon I should be able to hit a few Germans.'

Poverty as much as patriotism inspired many of the volunteers of 1914. Army pay, a little more than a parlourmaid's, was 8 shillings a week, plus keep, and a better deal, at least for an unmarried man, than the possible 13 shillings he might earn on a farm in Grundisburgh. That was a good rate (it was said to be 10 shillings in Swilland) and, despite the agricultural depression, was 50 per cent higher than the figure of 90 years earlier – slightly more now than a pair of boots rather than slightly less as previously.

It was the equivalent of about £30 today, if you exclude rent: in those days 18 pence per week was a typical rental, which in real terms is one-seventh of the £24.50 a week currently being charged by the Gurdon Trust to its subsidised tenants in Chapel Row, who of course also receive modern amenities. For 18 pence all you got were four walls and a roof. The half dozen or more children of many families would often share one bedroom, if not one bed. These conditions are remembered now with grim amazement, but they are the same in which people had lived for generations and would continue to do until the economic and social changes of the Second World War. Not least among such changes was farm mechanisation, which at last freed the workers who still remained on the land from the unending physical grind which had broken the bodies of so many of their ancestors.

The dreaded telegrams with their news from the battlefield were not Grundisburgh's first taste of war. As in Napoleonic times, two hundred or more troops were billeted in the village, Welsh vocalists and Scots bagpipers among them. The stench of army stores and cooking pervaded every requisitioned area (Baptists' schoolroom, the infants' room at the school, and the Parish Rooms) while on the green, military boots, horses and tents soon created a desert of dust or mud. Thatched Cottage was the Quartermaster's Stores, Miss Payne's house nearby (on the site of the present Rectory) an isolation hospital, and Finndale House a convalescent home.

Typhoid fever broke out at Finndale House, and the local girls who were its main connection with the village were warned off, to no effect: no one would admit to visiting the soldiers there, but it was a serious matter and two children had already died of the disease. P.C. Gray had to conceal his considerable bulk in a laurel bush near the house to catch a group of them red-handed.

Although Hugh Peche's Whitsun Fair had come to an end by the eighteenth century, fairs and circuses were regular visitors to Grundisburgh before the First World War, as to many other villages.

Vine Cottages about 1925. They were then sited in the present Rectory garden. Miss Payne's house (the wartime isolation hospital) is at the far end.

Here, outside the Dog, boxing contests were a feature, encouraged by the Rector whose sons were good at it. One hopes they met their match on the long-remembered day when a woman boxer appeared on the scene. Local women were used to more basic competitions, like straddling the stream or lying across it to make a dam.

The second Sunday in July was the Chapel Anniversary. Often a thousand people would come into the village for the special service – quite like the old days – overflowing onto the road dangerously close to the Sun, never the quietest of pubs, and the scene at such times of many a disedifying brawl. The Baptist annual Sunday school outing was no doubt more peaceful, a three-hour journey to Felixstowe in Foulger's horse-drawn wagons, later speeded up when Charles Cotton took them to Bealings station behind one of his traction engines.

Bell-ringing was a popular activity, rather surprising in the circumstances because in 1904, for the second time in the church's history, St. Mary's tower showed signs of crumbling. It was agreed the bells should only be rung briefly and on special occasions until the money was available to strengthen it. That was not until 1949, by which time the original embargo had been generally forgotten. The tower swayed quite visibly but no one worried.

The Brass Band was inhibited by no such problems. Under the leadership of Walter Blackmore, the schoolteacher, and subsequently of the motor-bus proprietor, Arthur 'Puffer' Cotton who played the trombone, they travelled the district by wagon or bus to play at church parades and similar events. The majority were tradespeople, not farm workers. The uniform was no doubt an added attraction: the first half of the twentieth century was uniform-mad.

Frederick Clarke, whose father in the 1870s had briefly been landlord of the Dog, was another prominent bandsman. In about 1890 Fred, who was a carpenter, built himself a working model windmill 25 feet high behind his house at the end of Maltings Lane. It was a smock mill ('smock mill or mock mill?' asked some reporter) whose operation is similar to that of a tower mill, rather than a revolvable post-mill, but made of wood not brick. The windmill survived into the Second World War, longer than the Barley Mow down the lane where in the 1920s his son Charles had been landlord, founder of the still-prospering building business.

The post-mill itself had been owned since about 1890 by the Nunns and occupied by their foreman, William Titshall. Robert Nunn died in 1929 and his widow hired Amos Clarke of Woodbridge to dismantle it. This other Mr. Clarke, who was originally a millwright, had discovered a little niche in his vanishing market, supplying scarce seasoned oak from the mills receiving his professional attention to satisfy the neo-Tudor craze for a wealth of exposed beams.

The Nunns were able to extract a profit from the mill by combining it with their corn merchant's shop at The Old Bakery, something no other family except the Forsdicks seems to have attempted. Mrs. Nunn had briefly tried her hand at selling bread as well, but Ann Hogger, in part of Folly Cottage opposite, appears to have become too well established as village baker since Charlotte Bays had retired from The Old Bakery itself in the 1870s.

Mrs. Hogger was followed as baker by Mrs Charles Foulger. Her husband, in addition to being a carrier and pork butcher, was also a dairyman and every Sunday would milk Cherry on the green to catch the customers on their way home from church. (Morning and evening in the summer, her descendants can still be seen ambling through the village). Milk, otherwise, was mostly delivered at 2 pence a pint from Lord Cranworth's prolific Red Polls of Elm Tree Farm.

Frederick Groom's shop, three doors up from the Foulgers, continued to sell meat until the 1930s when it switched to fish and chips. The best meat in the village, however, came from the shop near the Dog run for many years by Mrs. Leah Burch, Philip Harris's daughter. Behind it was the slaughterhouse (only very recently demolished) whither Cocky Howlett drove cattle on the hoof from Ipswich market. When he wasn't doing that, he sat on a tree trunk at

The Band outside the Old Bakery, Nunn's coal and corn merchant's shop. (The three at the front are: Harry Miller, Ernie Cook and Walter Leech. At the back: Arthur Cotton, Edwin Dunnett and H. Stannard.)

the bottom of Meeting Lane blowing a horn. Mrs Burch on her marriage had bought Brook Farm from the Bedwells; it contained not only what came to be known as Burch's meadow, the circus-site behind the Barley Mow, but also Bread Field, whimsically designated by Ben Bedwell as a reminder of the farm's obligation to Thinge's charity.

Arthur Savage on the green remained the village postmaster and principal grocer-cum-draper until his death in 1923, when he was succeeded by his daughter and son-in-law, the Lingleys. After the war, on Mrs. Lingley's death, the Post Office business was transferred up the hill to its present position.

At Hill House at the top of Rose Hill, the Stannards opened a newsagent's and florist's shop to which they later added cycles. They had previously been live-in assistants at Savage's, and set up on their own after Arthur got married in 1881. John Stannard was also a light harness maker, no competitor to George Reeve of Saddler's Cottage who specialised in farm horses. George, who died in 1956, had been Tom Reppington's apprentice and took over the house and business on his death in 1899, exactly as Tom himself had done with George Knight in the 1840s. Between the three of them, they span over 150 years.

The old trades were dying out. The 1891 census records only one shoemaker, once so numerous in Grundisburgh – John Lambert in

Fred Clarke's Smock Mill.

Woolnough's old shop at the bottom of Meeting Lane, and later at
Westholme opposite the Parish Rooms. The same census shows just
a single carpenter, who thought to mention he was also a wheel-
wright. The Pipes' basketmaking business closed for good in the
1970s; that was soon after Crapnell's forge had ben dispatched to the
Stowmarket museum, the last survivor of the five smithies (probably
more than there had ever been before) which amazingly had
provided a living in the village for much of the first half-century of
the motor-car: in addition to the three established ones, there was a
fourth up the hill in Stoney Road and a fifth at Rustic Cottage as an
adjunct to the Cooks' building business, which by now had expanded to include Meadowside next door.

In the interregnum between the death of old John Crapnell in the
1890s and the arrival of Fred in 1913, Crapnell's forge had been run
by Arthur Fosker. Fosker then started the forge half-way up Stoney
Road, further from the Dog where he was a valued customer.

Similarly the shops, around a dozen at the turn of the century,
were down to five by 1965. Meat and groceries, they said, even
when delivered to your door free of charge, were cheaper in
Woodbridge.

Hill Cottage near the top of Meeting Lane, between about 1910
and 1935, was Sister Flora Smith's Maternity Home. Sister Flora,
who was seldom seen out of uniform, was not cheap and served a
clientele extending well beyond the village, some of whom came to
her with an ulterior motive and left behind their unwanted babies for
adoption. If a doctor was required, one would come out from

Saddler's Cottage in Mr Reeve's time.

Woodbridge or Otley. There had been none in Grundisburgh since Dr. (or Mr.) Steggall, the former midwife, gave up general practice in his eighties around 1905. Otherwise there was another Smith, Julia of Rosmaree Cottage, hardworking, taciturn and much relied on, dispensing strange remedies whose origins were buried deep in the darkest period of the middle ages.

The Police Station, having moved down Rose Hill to one of the Dog cottages in the 1880s, had moved again to the other side of Bridge House by the time Ben Gray was in charge. After the Second World War it went back up the hill to Park Road between Pound Corner and the homes built earlier for the upper servants at the Hall.

By P.C. Gray's time the Pound, an institution of great antiquity, a lock-up with a well and fetid green pond for stray farm animals, was no more. No more, likewise, were the stocks and whipping-post on the village green, long since removed to the graffito-security of the Hall gardens.

A few yards down the hill, the Women's Institute in 1925 built themselves a hall on land donated by Lord Cranworth. It was really a gift to the village rather than the W.I. National Federation and the land was never legally conveyed, a nicety which came to a crisis during the building developments of the 1960s. Many women, who remembered their struggle to raise the original £639, were understandably incensed by the proposal, at length adopted, that, enlarged

Arthur Fosker at Crapnell's Forge, about 1910.

and modernised and without even priority of use for the W.I., their building should be taken over by the parish as a Village Hall. The fracas was made more poignant by the fact that the Chairman of the Parish Council and the President of the W.I. were husband and wife.

'Sealion', the German invasion plan, perished, as Churchill put it, in September 1940 after the Battle of Britain. Grundisburgh was not convinced, and in the summer of 1941 an invasion committee was set up under the chairmanship of Lord Cranworth. Food dumps and secure water supplies were organised, and sandbags, buckets, ladders and stretchers counted. Arrangements were discussed for digging a mass grave, a register established of women who could milk the cows (here was a potential crisis: there were only three) and an instruction pamphlet composed and delivered to every household.

The ringing of church bells was the universal warning of invasion, but it was important to guard against pranksters, so St. Mary's belfry was kept locked. Only the Rector, one air raid warden and the Home Guard C.O. held keys. Hopefully one of them would be around when the Germans came. In any case only the C.O. had authority actually to ring the bells, although P.C. Moody might do so in the special circumstance of his seeing personally a minimum of six enemy paras, and of course finding a key. It was all encouraged by

P.C. Moody, 'Sheriff' Moody to the U.S. airmen.

higher command for morale's sake, and assuredly great fun for the year it lasted.

Immediately after the war Pamela and George Lyttelton, a retired Eton schoolmaster, arrived in the village having purchased Finndale House, sight unseen. Posthumously, with the publication of the six volumes of letters which he had exchanged during his retirement with a former pupil, Rupert Hart-Davis, George put Grundisburgh after a thousand years on the world map. The letters became best-sellers and throughout the English-speaking world there are surely people today who may never have heard of Bury or Ipswich but who, thanks to Lyttelton, know something of Grundisburgh. (See Appendix.)

With the improvement in living standards after the war there came the concomitant anxieties of prosperity. Strangers, too, were better off and wanted the advantage of a house and garden in a village near, but not too near, their place of work. What had started as the construction of a few Council homes for returning war heroes in Stoney Road escalated by the 1970s into the 250 new houses of

Rebuilding Grundisburgh Hall, 1970.

Orchard End, Meeting Lane, Cranworth Close, Post Mill Gardens, and infilling elsewhere. In 30 years the population grew by 50 per cent to over 1,000; and the threat of a new access road via Town Lane, plus the size of the sewage works built beyond Lower Road in 1968, were clear warnings the authorities were prepared to contemplate that this figure itself might soon be doubled.

In 1972, as if to emphasise that this was not the case, a Policy Statement was published. Thirty years is almost a working lifetime to a planning officer but not much in the long evolution of a Domesday village. All that was wrong with the new blood was the speed with which it was being injected, a question the Policy Statement, with its jargon of focal points, distinctive buildings, floorscapes, wirescapes and areas of special control, never really addressed.

Perhaps for the first time since the arrival of Grundi (if he did arrive) Grundisburgh is referred to as a settlement. Some settlement, now larger than Norman Ipswich.

APPENDIX

———————❦———————

Extracts from George Lyttelton's Letters referring to local people and events

7 December 1955: Not that the diversions of Grundisburgh are very numerous – no huntin', shootin', or fishin', no Morris dancing, nor Knurr and Spell[1]. We could call on Mrs. Pizzey, we could talk to Mrs. Paternoster – oh no, I forgot, she is stone deaf. Charlie Balls has, alas, left the village. No coarse laughter from you, please. It is a very common name in Suffolk, so much so that at, say, a political meeting a loud shout of 'Balls' is usually not a comment on what is being said on the platform, but merely one of the clan hailing another across the hall. But there is always work of some kind in the garden – not much with the spade with which Wilkinson (*not* Lyttelton) had tilled his land, but with axe and saw. I hate the spade but love the axe. The fare is well enough and those who have tasted my wife's omlettes are convinced that even on the innermost recesses of Abraham's bosom they will find nothing better. We have no resident staff. A good woman comes in the morning; the gardener we share with another, but, thanks be, he lives next door, so lights the stove every day. There is a rather spacious garden with a stream, a revolving summerhouse which is warm whenever the sun shines, even in January, and where I spend many hours, writing and reading.

18 May 1956: Among my fortuitous but immensely precious circumstances I count almost the luckiest that when they began monkeying about with the game of bridge I couldn't be bothered to learn all the new stuff, so dropped out. If I had not, what aeons I should have wasted, e.g. in January at Brancaster, and here with the Cranworths, he having ceased to read and *must* be entertained. And one is very vulnerable in the country; they know one has no excuse – except that one doesn't want to!

27th August 1957: The Rector here prays every Sunday for fine weather, so far without visible result. How often August is a detestable month, but we forget it every year. An old friend of mine on the village green remembers the days before machinery when sometimes the harvest went on until November. He is over ninety and recently I came across him borrowing an *axe* from the blacksmith. He is a philosopher: 'They say there's nothing in the old Swithun; but I hain't often found him wrong'.

1. A 16th century north country game resembling trapball.

21 February 1957: I feel as foolish as I did last week when, standing at the bus-stop cross-roads, I signalled all clear to a van coming from Burgh into the Woodbridge-Tuddenham road at right-angles. A moment later there was a crash of ironmongery as a retired admiral in his Morris came down the W-T road like a driven grouse. Do you know the feeling of not having the smallest vestige of leg to stand on? It is most unpleasant. The only ray of comfort I got was the sight of both of them reduced, if not to equanimity, at least to almost complete silence by my admission that the whole thing was entirely my *fault*.

16 October 1957: Poor luck yesterday. In the bus to Ipswich I noticed a small child of extravagant plainness, its face, like that of Sulla in Plutarch, resembling 'a dish of mulberries sprinkled with flour'. I was recalling that lovely remark of Groucho Marx when someone said he hated to see a small boy crossing the street, 'I hate him anyvay.' This child sensed my feelings and retaliated suddenly by being sick – only just missing me, but in such cases a miss is as good etc. Shortly after the bus ran, rather wildly but with a good deal of splintering of glass, into a tree. Later on, after I had got out, I heard that a lady's shopping basket, into which she had thrown her cigarette, had caught fire.

17 September 1958: The family holidays here are just ending and Pamela and I return to our normal Darby and Joan existence. Last Sunday we filled three pews in the parish church, which made a considerable sensation among the worshippers. An elderly parson, known to be pretty gaga, was so staggered that he prayed for the Duke of Wales and Elizabeth the Queen Edinburgh, and later gave out that there would be no Communion service on the 58th of the month.

30 October 1958: Then – more local stuff – this evening I have to be Question-master at a clerical brains-trust in the village hall. I have looked through the questions, and shall find it rather hard to avoid a certain ribaldry. The questions are rather like those that Man Friday put to Robinson C. – and completely stumped him. You remember? 'Does God like the Devil?' 'No, he hates him.' 'But God can do anything?' 'Yes, certainly.' 'Then why doesn't God kill the Devil?' Why indeed? I expect I shall put my foot in it by betraying that I think either the lay question or the clerical answer ridiculous. We shall see.

5 November 1958: There was an element of comedy about the Grundisburgh Brains Trust. There were rather too many questions and a few were omitted which in my opinion and Pamela's were not of general interest or importance. I boiled one or two together and in the end only two were left out. Both had been sent in by our Rector! He rather stuffily wanted to know why, and I answered with truth and nothing but the truth that they were not on my paper, leaving him under the impression that somehow the slip on which he wrote them had gone astray. One question was why in the Communion epistle and gospel are now separated by a hymn, and the other was why do the R.C.s celebrate a different number of Sundays after Whitsun than does the C. of E. The panel had no idea that they did – and if you can think of a topic more completely empty of interest or moment I should like to hear it.

10 December 1958: Clerical ignorance of literature seems very common now. Our man here – he came only eight months ago – goes to another extreme. Last Sunday he referred to Karl Barth[1] and the Orphic myth,[2] without any explanation of either. Meanwhile half the unmarried young women are with child, and many of the marriages precede or follow the arrival of the firstborn by a matter of a few weeks or even days. Not necessarily as a sequel to the Orphic myth, as none of them comes to church. And after all East Anglia has always been noted for the trial trip before marriage, as in old days husbands, especially farmers, liked to know they would have families before committing themselves.

4 February 1959: I have had a nice little local *row*! Asked to contribute to a leaving present for a Woodbridge parson – unwillingly sent cheque for £1 – not acknowledged – wrote fortnight after to ask had it arrived – no answer – wrote to protest about discourtesy – organiser offended – and asked didn't I know that cheques need not be acknowledged nowadays – wrote glacially commenting on organisers regarding a contribution to a gift in same light as payment of tradesman's bill. No answer. There isn't one of course, but, alas, he has my £1. Bad manners make me positively waspish, nothing much else does. The organiser said he was not in the habit of being discourteous. I ought to have answered as Gussie Fink-Nottle[3] did when Tom Travers said he had never talked nonsense. 'Then, for a beginner, you do it dashed well.'

12 February 1959: Crossbills are unknown to me (not that that is odd) but also I believe unknown in Suffolk. Starlings are the devil; I was pleased to read that for some forgotten reason hundreds or even thousands of them died recently. Pigeons are a foul nuisance too in these parts. Do you see eye to eye with those who say *all* things are sent for our good? Our Rector is one of them . . .

Pamela is sitting at the Rector's feet listening to his lenten address – not because she wants to, but to swell his meagre audience. Last night she attended the Youth Club, merely because the good woman who runs it said no adult ever came. To-morrow we both go to hear a lecture on leprosy for a more mundane reason, viz. I have a morbid interest in leprosy.

21 May 1959: What a time you have had! Delirium one night? . . . Were you prayed for in Henley church? You would have been here; our Rector prays for people without being asked to, and once did so for an elderly gentleman

1. Swiss theologian (1886-1968).
2. Regarding pagan fertility rites.
3. In *Right Ho, Jeeves*, by P.G. Wodehouse.

who was present, some alarmist villager having said two days before that 'poor Mr. Barker had gone to hospital'. And so he had – to have an ingrowing toe-nail dealt with, or something equally unlethal . . .

The Yank family is ensconced over the old stables. Very friendly and happy. Pamela told them the orchard was the children's playground, but they never go near it, preferring the dusty little yard giving onto the road. I asked the four-year-old why they didn't go into the orchard and got the answer: 'There's chickens there; they might bite me.'

23 July 1959: A near neighbour of ours who lost her husband very suddenly a month ago had her house burnt down on Tuesday – 'Father-like He tends and spares us.' Nobody knows why, though wiseacres are pursing their lips and shaking their heads over a Russian maid, 'a chain-smoker of cigarettes' they say. The next house to this one has a thatched roof, and the owner of it and his wife are always in a dither about fire. I suppose you saw about the train which puffed fifteen miles to Felixstowe, followed by a fire engine. Pretty well every yard of the banks on the railway from here to London is black. And the heavens are as brass.

27 August 1959: I am in the summer-house – after a month during which it was far too hot. And of course this would be the day on which Pamela is turning me out of it and entertaining; and all the afternoon and evening the garden will be full of old women, led by a vivacious nonagenarian named Mrs. Shadrach Gray. She used to darn my socks and when I questioned her charge of one penny per sock as being absurdly small, she replied firmly that it was what she charged in 1897 and why should she change?

18 May 1960: All Lytteltons are hopeless ignoramuses about birds and flowers, but I like their names . . . We are not very rich in birds here, though I have a suspicion my ears may be partly to blame. But alas the nightingale has been banished from his old group of trees by building, and his note is distant and sounds discouraged.

25 May 1960: Any news about your shopkeeper is welcome. I hope her non-speak with the travelling baker is/are not only because of deafness. Those village animosities can be Olympian. Here Mr. Dunnett has not spoken to Mr. Willy Cook for seventeen years; Mrs. Patemorrer, though living next door to her, will deny to her last breath any knowledge of the existence of Mrs. Pizzey . . .

We have a new neighbour here, one Patrick Barrington who used to write excellent light verse in *Punch* and elsewhere. (Do you remember his pet hippopotamus which he nursed through hippopotameasles and hoppo-potamumps?) Last week he came to tea at 4.30 and left at 7.45 without once drawing breath. Pamela said it was my fault and I encouraged him in capping quotations etc.

1 June 1960: Comic about your Calverts (the chief factotum at Pamela's home Babraham was one William Calvert for years). It is much the same here; Pipes and Dunnetts swarm, all disclaiming any relationship with each other, though everyone knows they are connected, however different their social levels.

July 5 or 6, anyway Wednesday: You know, Rupert, the fundamental – and slightly depressing – difference between my letters and yours is that yours are full of interesting things you have done, and ditto people you have seen. I, having done neither, am reduced, largely, to not very inspiring chatter about what I have been reading . . . What can be done about it? Nothing that I myself can see. Shall I tell you what Miss Smith (nicknamed 'the Drip') said about teaching Eng. Lit. to girls who confuse Ben Jonson with Dr. Johnson and are not in the least abashed by her horror? Shall I tell you how I scored off the Inspector of Taxes last week, or that the reason why George Dunnett the local carpenter won't now go up a ladder, is not because at seventy-five, his balance (like mine) is untrustworthy, but because his weight being eighteen stone, he is sure that sooner or later a rung will wilt beneath his foot.

19 October 1960: It is very pleasant up here (Kirkby Lonsdale) and Pamela is having a grand rest from her numberless chores in Grundisburgh, where half the inhabitants' first idea is 'When in doubt about *anything*, send for Mrs. L.' The last before we left was from a woman whose husband had to go to hospital, and *would* dear Pamela just nip over and help her pack his clothes.

St. Andrew's Day 1960: We called on the Cranworths yesterday. He has (*aetat* eighty-three) also taken to a hearing-aid – of the type that *my* good man said was *not* now regarded as satisfactory. He doesn't like it (Lord C.) any more than I do mine, but I handed on, to his comfort, the unanimous testimony to the good results of use and patience. At present if anyone drops a pen I am deafened by the din, but hear much less well the human voice. However *my* comfort is that Pamela definitely says she no longer 'has to bellow like a bull' (wives *do* exaggerate you know) at our *tête-à-tête* meals, so all is not lost. Poor old Cranworth seemed to me to hear no better than before (such was his belief too) but I fear that often his brain was not taking much in. There would surely be literally nothing to be said against euthanasia if it wasn't for nears and dears.

11 May 1961: Slightly comic Governors' meeting of Woodbridge School yesterday. Next year we are to have tercentenary celebrations. What big noise shall we try to get? The Duke of Edinburgh? Well who do we approach to find out if he could or would? The Lord Chamberlain. Who is he? Lord Nugent. Does anyone know him? G.W.L.: 'My first pupil' – but he isn't the Lord Chamberlain. Who is? Eric Penn. Does anyone know him? G.W.L.: 'He was in my house', but he isn't the man. Some governor: 'No, the man to go for is Sir Edward Ford. Does anyone know him?' G.W.L.: 'He is my cousin.' Another governor: 'I believe the right man is Sir Michael Adeane; does anyone know him?' G.W.L.: 'He is my wife's cousin.'

Another: 'Suppose we can't get him. What about the Queen-Mother? Does anyone know her?' G.W.L.: 'She was a great friend, before marriage, of my wife's.'

So now I am in the eyes of my fellow-governors either *very* highly connected or the biggest snob in England.

23 November 1961: I had a glorious flop not long ago with a speech to the Old Boys of Ipswich – an entirely carnal and philistine crowd who had no interest at all in the history and traditions of the school but were wholly satisfied by such tales as what Smith mi said to the matron about the lavatory in 1944. A depressing evening, as I said to the Archdeacon of Suffolk who was also there. 'But you must remember,' he said, 'that they are all shop-keepers and sanitary inspectors, who have never heard of Cardinal Wolsey' (who is supposed to have founded the school – erroneously).

5 April 1962: George has asked me to write and say that he feels too ill to write any letters, but is most grateful to you for yours. At the moment he says he feels he can't cope with either receiving them or writing them. I am afraid he does feel horribly ill and I have an awful feeling that there is nothing they can do. We have not yet had the hospital report. Your friendship and letters have meant so much to George, I really can't tell you *how* much, and by the same token I do thank you so much for your sympathy and understanding. Love from Pamela.

25 April 1962: (Dictated to Pamela): There is nothing in anything except my gratitude and the wonderfulness of Pamela (she mustn't cross that out). So what then? I am not even a chaos – I am a vast infinity. She will write you any more, if there is anything. Love to Ruth and bless you both. Oh the boredom!

(He was suffering from cancer of the liver, and died on 1 May 1962.)

List of
Principal Sources Consulted

GENERAL

East Anglian Magazine.
East Anglian Miscellany.
Wendy Goult: A Survey of Suffolk Parish History (1990).
Grundisburgh Local History Magazine, 1984–1990.
E. Moor: Suffolk Words and Phrases (1823).
K.O. Morgan (ed.): Oxford History of Britain (1988).
W. Page (ed.): Victoria History of the County of Suffolk (1911).
J. Richardson: The Local Historian's Encyclopedia (1986).
J.M. Stratton: Agricultural Records 220–1968 (1969).
Proceedings of the Suffolk Institute of Archaeology.
The Suffolk Review.

CHAPTER ONE

W.G. Arnott: The Place Names of the Deben Valley Parishes (1946).
W.A. Copinger: The Manors of Suffolk (1905).
H.C. Darby: The Domesday Geography of Eastern England (1952).
R. Welldon Finn: Domesday Studies: The Eastern Counties (1952).
R. Welldon Finn: Domesday Book: A guide (1973).
A. Rumble (ed.): Domesday Book: Suffolk (1986).
F.M. Stenton: Anglo-Saxon England (1971).

CHAPTER TWO

V. Gibbs (ed.): The Complete Peerage (1910).
S.H.A. Hervey (ed.): Suffolk Subsidy Returns 1327–1568.
J.T. Munday: Early Medieval Eriswell (1965).
P. Palgrave-Moore: How to locate and use Manorial Records (1985).
E. Powell: The rising in East Anglia (1896).
N. Scarfe: Suffolk in the Middle Ages (1986).

CHAPTER THREE

Blois Papers.
J. Corder (ed.): The Visitation of Suffolk 1561 (1981).

Cranworth Papers.

Grundisburgh Manor: Surveys, Court Books and Minutes.

G.E. Mingay: English Landed Society in the eighteenth century (1963).

CHAPTER FOUR

H.R. Barker: East Suffolk Illustrated (1908).

J.H. Bettey: Church and Parish (1987).

E.J. Evans: Tithes and the Tithe Commutation Act (1978).

Grundisburgh Parish Records.

R.J.P. Cain and H.C. Prince: The Tithe Surveys of England and Wales (1985).

N.F. Layard: Seventeen Suffolk Martyrs (1902).

D.P. Mortlock: Popular Guide to Suffolk Churches (1990).

H. Munro Cautley: Suffolk Churches (1982).

S.L. Ollard and G. Crosse (ed.): A Dictionary of English Church History (1912).

V.B. Redstone: Memorials of Old Suffolk (1908).

J. and J.A. Venn (ed.): Alumni Cantabrigienses (1924).

H.F. Westlake: The Parish Guilds of Medieval England (1919).

CHAPTER FIVE

Baptists' Anniversary Booklet (1898).

Baptist Church Books and Registers.

A.K. Cowell: Mr. John Thompson (1827).

T.J. Hosken: History of Congregationalism in Suffolk (1920).

A.J. Klaiber: The Story of the Suffolk Baptists (1931).

CHAPTER SIX

Census Returns 1841–1891.

Coroners' Inquests for the Liberty of St. Etheldreda 1767–1858.

B. Flint: Suffolk Windmills (1979).

Grundisburgh Civil Parish Records.

Kelly's Directories for Suffolk.

Probate Records at Ipswich.

R. Simper: Woodbridge and Beyond (1972).

White's Directories for Suffolk.

CHAPTER SEVEN

J. Glynde: Suffolk in the Nineteenth Century (1856).

Grundisburgh Town Books.

Nacton Workhouse: Guardians' Minutes, Accounts and Registers.

J. Richardson: Looking at Local Records (1983).
S. and B. Webb: English Poor Law History (1927).

CHAPTER EIGHT

Digest of Suffolk Schools, 1818.
M.G. Jones: The Charity School Movement (1938).
Grundisburgh and Burgh School Board: Minute Books and Log Books.
Grundisburgh Village Club: Minute Books.
N. Longmate: The Workhouse (1974).
Returns of Schools in Civil Parishes, 1871.
St. John's Home: Minute Books.

CHAPTER NINE

W.G. Arnott: Suffolk Estuary (1950).
Observations on the Woodbridge-Debenham Turnpike, 1800.
Quarter Sessions Papers: Grundisburgh and Burgh bridge 1863–80.
S. and B. Webb: Story of the King's Highway (1913).

Index

of names and places in Suffolk

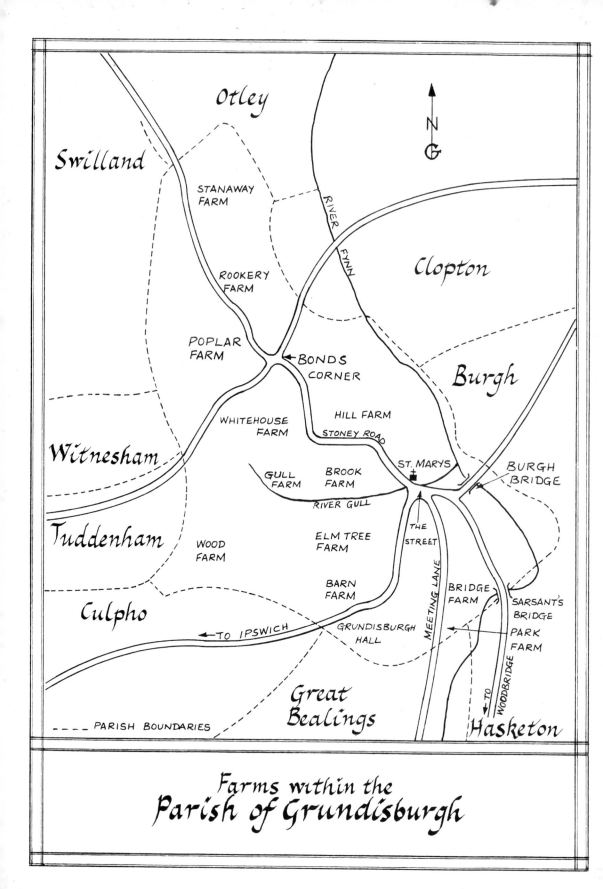

Farms within the
Parish of Grundisburgh